Numerology: Universal Vibrations of Numbers

This is a basic numerology workbook with work areas, examples, sample sheets, blank numerology forms, and numerology text. Because it is a workbook, it will show you how to complete a basic numerology chart simply and easily. This book was written to supply all the necessary tools to learn numerology step by step, so that you will pick up a working knowledge quickly.

The personal side of numerology is something everyone can use. Once the fundamentals are learned, numerology can be used as a guide in planning activities, making changes, or starting a project. In other words, this book can be used as a practical guide to everyday living.

When you learn and understand what digits are your main vibrations, you can direct your life with a more positive meaning. The more you know about the vibrations in your life, the more you will be able to map out a smoother, happier path.

Numerology offers a simple, complete, and efficient method of planning for the future—the best future.

"Barbara Bishop's book gives step-by-step instructions on setting up charts as well as detailed interpretations of the numbers' meanings. It provides an excellent explanation of why we encounter certain circumstances and conditions during our lifetimes, offering valuable information for the beginning student of numerology.

"Throughout the entire text the reader is aware of Barbara's dedication in bringing truth seekers to a deeper awareness of the Light within us all."

—**Daphna Moore**
International numerologist
and author of *The Rabbi's Tarot*

About the Author

Barbara Bishop believes she was put here for a purpose—to help people. An out-of-body experience in 1960 completely changed her thinking about life and death, bringing her to believe in a superior power: God.

Numbers have always played a part in Barbara's life and career choice—she has worked as an accountant, bookkeeper, and office manager. Her last job was as an over-the-road trucker, serving as relief driver for her husband.

In 1983, she taught herself how to operate and program a computer. She has written programs to formulate complete numerology birth charts. Because she wanted to teach numerology, she developed the format for this book.

In January, 1985, Barbara learned that she had been given the gift of auotomatic writing. Since then, she has gotten to know three family Spirit Guides, who have helped her to write this and other books.

To Write to the Author

If you wish to contact the author or would like more information about this book, please write to the author in care of Llewellyn Worldwide, and we will forward your request. Both the author and publisher appreciate hearing from you and learning of your enjoyment of this book and how it has helped you. Llewellyn Worldwide cannot guarantee that every letter written to the author can be answered, but all will be forwarded. Please write to:

Barbara Bishop
c/o Llewellyn Worldwide
P.O. Box 64383-056, St. Paul, MN 55164-0383, U.S.A.
Please enclose a self-addressed, stamped envelope for reply, or $1.00 to cover costs.
If outside the U.S.A., enclose international postal reply coupon.

Free Catalog from Llewellyn

For more than 90 years Llewellyn has brought its readers knowledge in the fields of metaphysics and human potential. Learn about the newest books in spiritual guidance, natural healing, astrology, occult philosophy and more. Enjoy book reviews, new age articles, a calendar of events, plus current advertised products and services. To get your free copy of *Llewellyn's New Worlds of Mind and Spirit*, send your name and address to:

Llewellyn's New Worlds of Mind and Spirit
P.O. Box 64383-056, St. Paul, MN 55164-0383, U.S.A.

NUMEROLOGY

UNIVERSAL VIBRATIONS OF NUMBERS

A NUMEROLOGY WORKBOOK
WITH TEXT AND BLANK FORMS

BARBARA J. BISHOP

1994
Llewellyn Publications
St. Paul, Minnesota 55164-0383, U.S.A.

FIRST LLEWELLYN EDITION
Third Printing, 1994

Cover Design by Christopher Wells
Book Design by Terry Buske and Jack Adair

Library of Congress Cataloging-in-Publication Data

Bishop, Barbara J.
      Numerology: universal vibrations of numbers / Barbara J. Bishop.
        p.   cm. — (Llewellyn's self-help series)
      ISBN 0-87542-056-7
      1. Numerology. I. Title. II. Series.
BF1623.P9B46   1990
133.3'35—dc20   89-77886
                                                                      CIP

Llewellyn Publications
A Division of Llewellyn Worldwide, Ltd.
P.O. Box 64383, St. Paul, MN 55164-0383

LLEWELLYN'S SELF-HELP SERIES

We all search for ways to succeed in our lives. The success we search for in business, relationships, self-image, and other areas often depends on information. One of the most often used methods of finding information which will guide us to greater success is through feedback. We often request feedback from friends, relatives, and co-workers and then attempt to sort out what is factual and what might be highly colored by the feedback-giver.

Employers often call their feedback "constructive criticism." Sometimes it is constructive and sometimes it is not. However, whether the feedback is constructive or not, one of the most valuable tools we have for greater success is information leading to self-awareness. With such information we can begin to change some of the aspects of our personality that have impeded our progess.

One of the books in Llewellyn's Self-Help Series is *Numerology: The Universal Vibrations of Numbers.* Numerology is a made-to-order key to opening our inner selves and exploring options for behavior change. With practice, one can make numerology an objective method of giving feedback to oneself. *It is important to be aware that it is possible for explorers of personal behavior to close their eyes to obvious deficiencies or defeating behaviors in themselves unless a truly open mind is kept.* Using the insights of numerology explained in this book can provide the reader with the means to acquire that most important of analytical tools—unbiased feedback.

Once the reader has discovered and accepted that important information, she/he can take steps to change behavior with the goal of personal success. Numerology offers an unbeatable channel to continue monitoring personal progress toward success.

DEDICATION

There is no way that I can take full credit for this book. First of all I give my thanks to GOD for the Special Gift HE bestowed upon me. I first became aware of Divine guidance and help through three Guides from my family, Warren, Freda, and Marcy, and from other special Spirit Guides who use only initials. They are given my special thanks because they helped me to write the first version of this book.

To my husband, Loren. Without his love, patience, understanding, and interest this book would not have been possible. He never complained when I started my day at 1 A.M. or worked past midnight. He helped me in may ways so that I would not have to stop when everything was running along smoothly for me. He spent many hours as my proofreader—reading and rereading. His faith and encouragement are wonderful. To you I dedicate this (our) book. Thank you, my love!

TABLE OF CONTENTS

ABBREVIATIONS

The following abbreviations are used in this book. Some may be used without the periods.

B.D.	Birth Digit
CHAL	Challenge or Challenges
D.	Day
EXP. or EXPR.	Expression
MO.	Month
P. of L.	Path of Life
P.D.	Personal Day
P.H.	Personal Hour
P.M.	Personal Month
P.Y.	Personal Year
Q.S.	Quiet Self
S.U.	Soul Urge
U.D.	Universal Day
U.H.	Universal Hour
U.M.	Universal Month
U.Y.	Universal Year
Y.	Year

Introduction

NUMEROLOGY is the ancient study of the meanings of numbers using a date or name, or both. It tells you which numbers are vibrating in your life, when they are in effect, and what the vibrations could mean. Numerology can tell you many different things about your personal life, business, or world and universal affairs. It will show you the path your life takes and the sub-paths or branches from that path, including your high points and challenges.

The object of this book is to teach the mathematics and basic interpretations used in numerology. It is in workbook form to make it easier to learn the procedures needed to find the correct numbers or digits used to complete a numerology chart. The philosophy of life implied in the text is that when life is lived with a positive attitude and in a positive way, things move along smoothly; but that when there are negative vibrations, things get rougher. The text in the definition sections will help you to recognize what positive and negative vibrations are. By checking what could be the vibrations you are obtaining, you have the power in your hands to change any negativity to a positive or better way of life. Some negative vibrations are listed with the hope of helping those who have that type of vibration to realize it, and to show them how it is possible to change to the positive way so that life becomes smoother for them. Life was meant to be lived in a positive manner.

"We," as used in this book, refers to material written by my Spirit Guides. "We" means what *they* say. We invite you to use this book with the intended purpose and spirit in which it was written. This book was written with you in mind, and its purpose is to teach the basics of numerology.

How to Use This Workbook

The first section is the work area. It will teach you how to find and use the correct single digit or Master Number combinations used in numerology. The exact name (from the birth certificate) and birth date are needed. These two facts determine what you are, what you have to work with, what your desires and dreams are, and the means to understanding and solving your problems.

Part I of the workbook section uses the birth date and some numerology functions based on that date. In Part II the numeric values, meanings and uses of the letters in the full name are shown. Part III uses a combination of both the date and name and gives other numerology information. Most sections will give an example and a worksheet-like format with space for your use, teaching how to do the figuring in the fastest and easiest way, starting with the birth date and the Path of Life.

In the Appendices section, Appendix A has the interpretation text pertaining to the numbers. You will find the keywords, aspects (positive, negative or destructive), general meanings of each number, and a list of occupations each number vibrates. Appendix B has the text for the alphabet values and meanings. Appendix C contains the blank numerology forms for use if you do not wish to write in the main textbook areas. These blanks will cover most of the work explained in this book.

On page 4 following the Introduction is a blank numerology chart worksheet to transfer the major digits you will be figuring in the work area (or use scratch paper if you prefer), and on page 5 is an example of that chart filled out using a fictitious birth date and name. The sample chart is for your use as a quick reference to proper placement of the name, date and other numbers. (The Personal numbers for the year, etc., are explained in the work area and are not on the sample chart.) Sometimes it will be easier to refer to this chart instead of thumbing back through the workbook looking for certain digits and/or examples.

The word *digit*, as used throughout this book, means one single number. Reduce all numbers to a single digit between 1 and 9 except 11 and 22 when they are found in major places such as the Path of Life, Soul Urge and the Expression. The numbers 11 and 22 are called Master Numbers. They have special meanings and sometimes must be reduced to a single digit because Master Numbers are too hard to live up to for some persons. Judge which way to use these when you construct and read someone's chart. Always write them as 11/2 or 22/4 to denote both possibilities, and read both options when checking the meanings or interpretations. Do not try to force a number to add to 11 or 22 if it really isn't there. The right numbers needed for a correct interpretation are all that you are looking for. Everything goes in cycles from 1 to 9, as the number 9 is the ultimate number in numerology and the Universe.

Each number has a positive and a negative meaning:

Positive: used to expand and understand, with confidence and certainty.

Negative: obstacles and consequences of our own pessimistic actions.

Also remember to be sure to look at the subtotals or the numbers behind the digits. Take them into consideration, too, as they may indicate a vibration or missing link needed. Keep in mind that the higher the number, the greater emphasis that number will be vibrating. A number 10 has stronger vibrations than a number 1, and a number 20 has stronger vibrations than a number 2, etc.

When it was written, this workbook was intended for use by those who wanted to learn by themselves, but now we realize it can be used by teachers of numerology also.

Some of the section titles in this book have additional title names in parentheses behind them. These are names used by other authors but they mean the same thing. Take the Path of Life, for example: some numerologists call it the Birth Force. The names are placed in this manner to help you when you are reading numerology books using the other names. Numerologists need to standardize these names.

I hope this book will help you to learn numerology faster and that all the methods used to find the correct digits will be easier for you to understand because of the worksheets and examples. When you have learned how to figure the digits and have used the keywords enough to remember them, you will find that you can use numerology for almost everything.

WORKSHEET

Use single digits only.

Birth Date: _____   Name:_____

    Month   _____   Formative Cycle   _____

    Day   _____   Productive Cycle   _____

    Year   _____   Harvest Cycle   _____

                _____Path of Life

                              Birth Day Vibrations   _____

Birth Digit   _____   Day Challenges   _____

                              Day Gift   _____

Life's Challenges: _____ Major _____ 1st Minor _____ 2nd Minor _____ Added

Year	(Age)	Path of Life	Life Cycles	Attainments or Pinnacles	Life's Challenges	Name Vibs.	Name Challenge
	Birth (3) (6) (9)				Major	Expr	Exp Chal
	(18)					S.U.	SU Chal
	(27)				First Minor	Q.S.	QS Chal
	(36)					First Vowel	
	(45)				Second Minor		
	(54)					Reality Number	
	(63)				Added Minor		
	(72)						
	(81)						
	(90)						

4

SAMPLE WORKSHEET

This is a sample worksheet using a fictitious name and birth date.

Birth Date: 11/20/1938   Name: George Lester Whiteside

Year	(Age)	Path of Life	Life Cycles	Attainments or Pinnacles	Life's Challenges	Name Vibs.	Name Challenge
1938	Birth	7	11/2	4	Major 1	Expr 4	Exp Chal 3
	(3)						
	(6)						
	(9)					S.U. 9	SU Chal 0
	(18)						
	(27)				First Minor 0	Q.S. 4	QS Chal 3
1967/8			(30)	(29) 5		First Vowel 5	
	(36)		2				
1976				(38) 9	Second Minor 1		
	(45)						
1985				(47) 5			
	(54)					Reality Number 11/2	
1995			(57)		Added Minor "None"		
	(63)		3				
	(72)						
	(81)						
	(90)						

SU digits: 7   +   1   +   1   =   9 SU
SU subtotals: 16   10   28
VOWELS: 5 6   5   5   5   9   5   9   5

FULL NAME: G E O R G E   L E S T E R   W H I T E S I D E
NUMERIC VALUES: 7 5 6 9 7 5   3 5 1 2 5 9   5 8 9 2 5 1 9 4 5

EXPR subtotals: 39   25   48
EXPR digits: 3   +   7   +   3   = 13 = 4 EXPR

CONSONANTS: 7   9 7   3   1 2   9   5 8   2   1   4
QS subtotals: 23   15   20
QS digits: 5   +   6   +   2   = 13 =   4 QS

PART I

Using The Birth Date

The Path of Life (Birth Force)

The Path of Life is what you were sent to Earth with, what you are to do, what your nature is, what talents you have, and what you are really like. This is your nature, your road in life. If this number is lived in a positive, optimistic manner, you could reach your goal successfully. If lived in a pessimistic way, there could be adverse reactions.

The Path of Life is the single digit number found by using the birth date. (In astrology the birth time is considered very important when making a correct chart. In numerology, the only time that I question is if someone were born around midnight during a Daylight Savings Time period. If someone were born between midnight and one A.M. Daylight Savings Time, their Universal date is actually the day before. In such a case, the time should be verified, because it could change the birth date and all the other places where the correct date is needed. I prefer to use Universal time, or as some call it, Local Mean time.)

Add the month of birth number, the day of birth number, and the year of birth. Reduce these to a single digit unless it is an 11 or a 22. These are Master Numbers and are not reduced when found on the Path of Life *unless* their vibrations are too hard for that person to live up to.

Using the birth date, the Path of Life is worked like this:

Month + Day + Year
To be added as:

Month	1–12 (January = 1, February = 2, etc.)
Day	1–31
Year	<u>4 digits</u>
Sum to be totaled as	# # # # = # # = Path of Life #.

Our example will use the birth date of our fictitious man, George.

November 20, 1938 will be added like this:

Month of Birth	11
Day of Birth	20
Year of Birth	<u>1938</u>
Total and reduce	1969 = 25 = 7 Path of Life.

1969 should be totaled as 1 + 9 + 6 + 9 = 25 = 2 + 5 = 7 Path of Life.

Now it is your turn to find the Path of Life. Fill in the blanks.

Month of Birth	(1–12)
Day of Birth	(1–31)
Year of Birth	+_____ (four digits)
Total and reduce	_____ = __ + __ + __ + __ = ____
	= __ + __ = ____ P. of L.

Now turn to the worksheet in the front of this book. Fill in the birth date and the name. Most students use their own name because it is the one that they are the most familiar with, but you may use any that you wish. Next fill in the month, day, and year and the Path of Life. The rest of the worksheet will be filled in at different times throughout this book.

PATH OF LIFE INTERPRETATIONS

The following pages define numerous vibrations for each number on the Path of Life. Also refer to the keywords and the number meanings in Appendix A.

1

Individuality is the key word on this path. You are the pioneer, the original, the creative one. You are a leader and not a follower, so you do better in a business for yourself or as a manager, foreman, or director. You do not like to take orders. You are ambitious, very determined, and unconventional. You lead a very active life. You are honest, loyal, and have a good sense of humor. You have self-assurance, pride, will power, and the ability to get things done. Guard against these negative vibrations: egotism, arrogance, boastfulness, selfishness and laziness.

2

Cooperation is the key word on this path. You work better in partnerships and groups. The 2 needs companionship. You are a good mixer. You are kind and thoughtful of others. Your success comes from helping others without expecting a reward, but you must be on guard so that you do not become their doormat. You are a peacemaker and a diplomat. You have a fine sense of rhythm. You usually marry. You are fond of detail and minuteness in your work. You prefer to stay in the background and are sometimes very shy. Home and family are important to you. Guard against these negative vibrations: refusing to accept help from others, oversensitivity, timidity, inability to take risks, and self-depreciation. You need to create will power and courage.

3

Pleasant is the key word on this path. You are enthusiastic, happy, creative, intuitive, imaginative, versatile, and energetic. You are intellectual, optimistic, and a natural leader. You must express yourself often, as you have a gift with words. It may be expressed in speaking, writing, acting, or singing. You have a good imagination and use it creatively. You are intuitive and do your best with mental work. You are friendly, and your friends mean a lot to you. You want beauty, joy, and happiness all around. You come up with new and original ideas to solve your problems. You should follow your hunches. Guard against these negative vibrations: overcriticalness, impatience, gossiping, jealousy, lack of self-esteem, and intolerance.

4

Organized and *practical* are the key words on this path. You are honest, sincere, serious, dignified, patient, and conscientious. You are the maker of the permanent and the lasting. You take responsibilities, and others ask for your support and protection. You build from the ground up. You desire order and regularity in work and at home. Detail means a lot to you, but sometimes you can be too exacting. You work on the intellectual plane. You are mechanically minded and work well with your hands. You are a hard worker. You are dependable, methodical, systematic, and orderly. You like to save money. You love home. Those with 4's are the foundation makers and should start with a solid base. You will work for your money and should not gamble. Guard against these negative vibrations: bossiness, hypercriticism, domineeringness, laziness, impatience, undependability, being a workaholic, or one who likes to have their own way.

5

Freedom is the key word on this path. You like to be free to come and go as you please. You are active, restless, impatient, a quick thinker, and like variety. You have many (sometimes too many) irons in the fire. Your opportunities come from dealing with the public. You want to try new things, go new places, meet new people, and try new jobs. Routine is very boring to you. You must be versatile. You are a good mixer and you make friends easily. The new and untried fascinates you to the point of trying everything at least once, but you learn from all of these experiences. You are a stickler about law and order. You must be careful about scattering your energies, time, and money, as this will leave things undone and others will think you are undependable. Your talents could be wasted if you become a victim of drink, dope, or sex. Do not get in a rut, as your opportunities are away from the beaten path, away from the routine of home and regular lines of work. Guard against these negative vibrations: irresponsibility, thoughtlessness, overindulgence in the senses (drink, dope and sex), and undependability.

6

Responsibility is the key word on this path. You must learn to serve others, to give counsel freely, to do good for all humankind without involving personal or selfish interests. You like your surroundings to be comfortable, peaceful, harmonious, musical, and beautiful. You are sympathetic, an idealist, frank, just, and a peacemaker. You may be blind to the faults of your loved ones. You prefer to work with others. Most 6's marry, but some set such a high standard for marriage that they feel they cannot live up to it and may marry late in life or not at all. Your home and family mean everything to you, and you like to have it revolve around you. You are artistic and like the beauty of nature, flower gardens, and a well-landscaped home. You have a keen sense of right and wrong. You care for the young, the old, and the weak. You are the humanitarian, the teacher, and often the doctor. You thrive in situations with responsibility and trust. Your success comes in all occupations connected with the home, institutions, community, or education. You give a helping hand when needed. Guard against these negative vibrations: pride, callousness, jealousy, meddlesomeness, stubbornness, domineeringness, and unreasonableness.

7

Wisdom is the key word on this path. You are one who seeks knowledge. You study, test, prove, and gain facts about the unknown, unseen, or the unproven. You delve into the mysteries of life. You are observing and analytical. You don't take others' word as gospel, so you dig deep to gather all the facts. The 7 is the number of the loner, and you will find yourself alone a lot of the time; but you put this time to good use by reading, thinking, studying, exploring, or inventing. You make a few chosen friends. You should mix with the thinkers of the world. The mysteries of the spiritual or metaphysical world fascinate you. You dislike manual labor. You need to share with others to find true happiness. The 7 could be a professor, teacher, or writer, etc. You must bring yourself out of the background and share your knowledge with the world. Leadership and partnerships are not for you. You are a mystery to others, which makes you misunderstood and unappreciated. Your success comes in professional lines of work. You are patient, self-confident, poised, intuitive, and have psychic abilities. Guard against these negative vibrations: impatience, melancholia, indifference, alcohol addiction, secretiveness, aloofness, and laziness.

8

Achievement is the key word on this path. This path is not an easy one, and success comes through knowledge, financial effort, and determination. It will come through your own effort when a balance is struck between the spiritual and the material without sacrificing personal satisfaction for monetary rewards. You must learn to work for the good of all rather than for yourself. This is when you will be rewarded. How you manage your money can make or break you. You prefer to lead, not to follow, so you most likely own a business or direct, manage, or supervise one. Big business attracts you because you do things in a big way. You need good judgment, courage, sound principles, ambition, and a lot of effort to attain your goal. Business persons, writers, literary people, and news correspondents should be among your friends. You may find yourself in education, finance, shipping, buying, selling, consulting, transportation, or charitable work, all on a large scale. You have executive ability. You are a good talker. The metaphysical interests you. Guard against these negative vibrations: excessive ambition for self and wealth, intolerance, abuse of power, selfishness, wastefulness, miserliness, extravagance.

9

Compassion is the key word on this path. You have the tolerance and understanding needed for your life of service to humankind. People in all walks of life turn to you. Your rewards come when you learn that service is your duty. You must help, inspire, and counsel others. You could lose if you demand power, possessions, and personal love, because your way of life requires that you remain impersonal. You seek perfection in yourself and others. You become disappointed and have a hard time understanding when others do not reach the perfection that you expect in them. You must learn that others have their own way in this life and that you cannot expect them to live up to your ideals. You are intellectual, talented, sympathetic, inspirational, intuitive, and generous. You will have many emotional experiences. There will be constant tests for compassion and the love of others. Your success comes through your selfless service to and the understanding of humankind. This could be through work in some kind of charity, in hospitals, in institutions, or in other nonprofit organizations. Do great things with your talents for the benefit of all, and you will be well rewarded. Guard against these negative vibrations: selfishness, unkindness, being unethical, miserliness, moodiness, timidity, uncertainty, and vacillation.

11

Inspiration is the key word on this path. This is a Master Number, and much is expected of you. You belong before the public and in the limelight. This could be as a lecturer, minister, diplomat, ambassador, critic, or spiritual adviser along metaphysical lines. You are intuitive, intelligent, artistic, a philosopher. You are an idealist. You have psychic abilities. Personal ambitions could be your downfall because your success comes through your knowledge, inspiration, revelation, and leadership to humankind. Your example of living inspires others, so make it the truth that has been revealed to you. You could be an artist, scientist, teacher, writer, reformer, healer, psychologist, peacemaker, or be employed in any line that helps and inspires others. Guard against these negative vibrations: conceit, dishonesty, selfishness, aimlessness, unkindness, indifference, and unconcern.

The Master Number 11 is the vibration for only a handful of people. When it feels right you will know that this is your number. Never force an 11. If this vibration feels incorrect for your life, refer to the number 2. This is not a reflection upon anyone with an 11/2 Path of Life. Master Numbers should never be forced. You need to know that there is an alternative for you.

22

Universal is the key word on this path. This is a Master Number and must give service on a large scale. This is the number of the master builder, architect, engineer, or anyone involved in large ventures that benefit groups of people or the world. Your interest lies in large cooperatives, world affairs, or international concerns. You do everything in a big way. Your best work is before or for the public. You can assume leadership, manage, and direct. You are not a follower. You may be a college or university professor, a teacher, a statesman, or other public benefactor. Your views should be universal, not personal, as you must contribute to the general welfare of humankind. Guard against these negative vibrations: nerves, excess, laziness, self-promotion, get-rich-quick schemes, mental turmoil, boastfulness, indifference.

This Master Number also has an alternative. If the 22 is too hard to live up to, look to the 4 Path of Life. Never force a number to add up to the Master Numbers. If they are not there, they do not belong there.

Life Cycles (Sub-Paths)

There are three sub-paths known as the Life Cycles, crossroads, or branches from the main Path of Life. They are the FORMATIVE CYCLE, the PRODUCTIVE CYCLE, and the HARVEST CYCLE. These cycles are secondary paths giving added opportunities to progress and acquire knowledge.

The Formative Cycle represents the informative years of life, the beginning that teaches. This is when life's foundation is put into place. The Productive Cycle is your work cycle, the time when you are the most productive. The Harvest Cycle is the time in life to reap or harvest the rewards of your past labors or deeds. If your life is lived to the best of your ability and positively, this should be a pleasant time for you. The ones that enjoy the Harvest Cycle the most are the ones who planned ahead in the Productive Cycle to make the Harvest Cycle rewarding and satisfying.

FORMATIVE CYCLE DIGIT   This is the same as the birth month digit.

formula: birth month (1–12) reduced to a single digit.

We are working our samples with George's birth date of November 20, 1938. Using the samples as a guide, place your dates in the work blanks. Example: 11 (birth month) = 1 + 1 = 2 or 11/2 Master Number.

FORMATIVE CYCLE = ____ (birth month) = ____ + ____ = _____.

PRODUCTIVE CYCLE DIGIT   The same as the birth day digit.

       formula: birth day (1–31) reduced to a single digit.

    Example: 20 (birth day) = 2 + 0 = 2.

PRODUCTIVE CYCLE = _____ (birth day) = ____ + ____ = _____ .

HARVEST CYCLE DIGIT   Same as the birth year digit.

      formula: birth year (four digits) reduced to a single digit.

    Example: 1938 (birth year) = 1 + 9 + 3 + 8 = 21 = 2 + 1 = 3.

HARVEST CYCLE = _____ (birth year) = __ + __ + __ + __ =

                                ___ = __ + __ = _____ .

NOTE: The total of all three cycles equals the Path of Life digit.

    Turn to the worksheet on page 4 and write the cycle digits that you have figured here directly under the Name (see the example below). The Life Cycles text in this section holds the meanings for the Life Cycle digits.

    Example
Name: George Lester Whiteside
      FORMATIVE CYCLE   11/2   (11 is a Master Number)
      PRODUCTIVE CYCLE   2
      HARVEST CYCLE   3

    Each Life Cycle has its own length of time. Where the Formative Cycle ends, the Productive Cycle begins. Where the Productive Cycle ends, the Harvest Cycle begins. The Formative Cycle runs from birth to approximately the 27th birthday, when the Productive Cycle begins. The Productive Cycle goes on to roughly the 57th birthday, when the Harvest Cycle begins. The Harvest Cycle extends through the rest of the life.

    To find the year in which the Life Cycles begin and end, you find a number 1 PERSONAL YEAR nearest the indicated age. (The new cycle *begins* on the birthday in a 1 Personal Year.) To find a Personal Year digit for any given year, you will need a UNIVERSAL YEAR digit and a BIRTH digit.

A Universal Year digit is found by reducing the year number in question to a single digit. For example: $1 + 9 + 8 + 3 = 21 = 2 + 1 = 3$ Universal Year (U.Y.).

Place the year number you will be using here _____ and reduce.

$1 + 9 + $ ____ $ + $ ____ $ = $ ____ $ = $ ____ $ + $ ____ $ = $ ____ U.Y.

To find a Birth digit you add the birth month to the birth day and reduce that total to a single digit if need be (see George's example below).

Birth Month   11
Birth Day   +20___
Total and reduce $31 = 3 + 1 = 4$ Birth digit (B.D.)

Find your Birth digit by filling in the blanks below.

Birth Month   _____

Birth Day   +_____

Total and reduce   _____ $ = $ ____ $ + $ ____ $ = $ _____ B.D.

Place the Birth digit on the worksheet in the front of the book. We will be using the Birth digit quite often from now on.

To find any Personal Year digit, add the Birth digit to the Universal Year digit of the year in question. Total and reduce (B.D. + U.Y. = P.Y.). The example to find the Personal Year digit for 1983 for George is below.

Birth digit   4   (use single digits only)
U.Y. digit   +3__ (using 1983)
Total and reduce $7 = 7 + 0 = 7$ Personal Year (P.Y.) digit.

To find your Personal Year digit, add your Birth digit to the Universal Year digit that you figured above.

Birth digit   _____

U.Y. digit   +_____

Total and reduce   ____ $ = $ ____ $ + $ ____ $ = $

_____ Personal Year (P.Y.) digit.

FINDING THE YEAR THE FORMATIVE CYCLE ENDS

Using the method to find a Personal Year digit outlined above, we will figure out the year the Formative Cycle ends. The Formative Cycle begins at birth and ends on the birthday in the 1 Personal Year nearest the 27th birthday. Some will find this cycle goes into their 30s.

Add the year of birth to the age of 27 and reduce (see example).

Year of Birth	1938	(using all four numbers)
Add age 27	+ 27	
Reduce	1965	= 1 + 9 + 6 + 5 = 21 = 2 + 1 = 3 U.Y.

Note that these digits are added only to get year numbers, so they are Universal Year numbers. This single digit number (U.Y.) is added to the Birth digit (B.D.) number, which is then reduced to a single Personal Year (P.Y.) digit. See the exmple below.

U.Y.	3	(1965, year George will be age 27)
B.D.	+ 4	(George's Birth digit)
Add. Reduce.	7	= 7 + 0 = 7 Personal Year (P.Y.) in 1965.

If not a 1 Personal Year (P.Y.) and the number is 5 or more, *ADD* the number of *YEARS* needed to reach the 1 P.Y. If the number is a 4 or less, *SUBTRACT* the number of *YEARS* need to reach the 1 P.Y. You need the 1 P.Y. nearest the 27th birthday. This is the year the Formative Cycle ends and the Productive Cycle begins. You will also need to adjust the age if you added or subtracted for the Personal Year. The corrected age will be the age reached (on the birthday) during the Universal Year where the 1 Personal Year number was found.

In our example for George, his Personal Year for age 27 (in 1965) was the digit 7. So we need to add three years to his age and three years to 1965. In 1968 George was in the 1 Personal Year nearest to his 27th birthday. This was the year (1968) and age (30) that his Formative Cycle ended.

Fill in the blanks below with your numbers.

Year of Birth	(use all four numbers)
Add age 27	+27
Reduce	_____ = ___ + ___ + ___ + ___ =
	_____ = ___ + ___ = _____ U.Y.

Add this U.Y. digit to the Birth digit to find the Personal Year.

          U.Y.

      B.D. + _____

Total and reduce. _____ = ____ + ____ = _____ P.Y.

      Use the space below to add or subtract the years needed if not a 1 Personal Year.

THE PRODUCTIVE CYCLE

The duration: If it begins before age 27, the full effect will not be felt until the 27th birthday. If after age 27, the full effect is not felt until the actual cycle is entered. The cycle starts on the birthday in the 1 Personal Year nearest age 27.

In our example for George, the Productive Cycle began November 20, 1968.

The cycles' durations are worked out by finding the beginning of the next cycle (by locating the 1 Personal Year nearest the age needed for that cycle). We worked out the end of the Formative Cycle and found the beginning of the Productive Cycle, which starts on that same birthday.

Working out the beginning of the Harvest Cycle will also show you the end of the Productive Cycle.

FINDING THE YEAR THE HARVEST CYCLE BEGINS

The duration: begins on the birthday in a 1 Personal Year nearest age 57, and is in effect through the rest of the life.

You find the year the Harvest Cycle begins in the same way that was used to find the end of the Formative Cycle or the beginning of the Productive Cycle, only this time we are looking for the 1 Personal Year nearest the 57th birthday.

Our example will find George's 1 P.Y. nearest age 57.

$$\begin{array}{ll} \text{Year of Birth} & 1938 \\ \text{Add age 57} & +\ \ 57 \\ \hline \text{Reduce.} & 1995 = 1 + 9 + 9 + 5 = 24 = 2 + 4 = 6\ \text{U.Y.} \end{array}$$

The Universal Year digit (U.Y.) is added to the Birth digit (B.D.)

$$
\begin{array}{lll}
\text{U.Y.} & 6 & \text{(1995. The year George reaches age 57.)} \\
\text{B.D.} & +\ \underline{4} & \text{(George's Birth digit.)} \\
\text{Reduce} & 10 & = 1 + 0 = 1\ \text{P.Y.}
\end{array}
$$

In this case, in 1995 and at age 57 George will be in a 1 Personal Year.

If this digit had been a 7, for example, we would have added 3 to both his age and the year date; if it had been a 4, we would have subtracted 3. Make any necessary adjustments to bring the Personal Year to the 1 Personal Year nearest the 57th birthday, just as we did in the example for George to find the end of the Formative Cycle. (Remember that when you are looking for the beginning of the cycle, the word *beginning* tells you that you are looking for a number 1 digit.)

Because the birthday in this year is the beginning of the Harvest Cycle, the day before was the ending of the Productive Cycle.

Fill in the blanks below with your numbers to find out the date when the Harvest Cycle begins.

Year of birth

Add age 57   + _57_

Reduce   = __ + __ + __ + __ = __ P.Y.

Add Universal Year digit to Birth digit.

U.Y.

B.D.   + ____

Reduce   = ____ + ____ = _____ P.Y.

If not a 1 P.Y., ADD or SUBTRACT the number of years needed in the space below. This same number of years also needs to be added or subtracted to correct the age.

Turn to the worksheet on page 4. We will now begin placing the most important digits used in numerology in the chart section. Notice that I have filled in the (AGE) column. (I bracket the ages with parentheses to distinguish them from other numbers in the chart.) Starting with birth, the ages advance down the column in progressions of three years for each row across and are written out for every nine years after the age of nine. Using the age numbers as a gauge, we will place the correct year numbers, numerology digits, and ages when the Cycles begin taking effect in their proper columns in even rows across the chart. To do this, use a ruler or straight edge to draw a line across the appropriate columns in each row where the years and ages match up. The years and ages will be placed above the lines, and the numerology digits will be placed below them. In this way you will be able to tell at a glance in what year and at what age the Cycles and Attainments change.

For example, using George's chart below, we see that in the top row his year of birth is 1938, his Path of Life is 7, and his Formative Cycle digit is the Master Number 11/2. Moving down to the year 1968, we look across the row to the Life Cycles column and see that his Productive Cycle begins at age 30 (in 1968) and that his Productive Cycle digit is 2. Farther down, we see that in 1995 his Harvest Cycle begins at age 57 and the Harvest Cycle digit is 3.

Following this example, place the digits you have worked out so far and their years in the proper places on your worksheet.

Year	(Age)	Path of Life	Life Cycles	Attainments or Pinnacles	Life's Challenges	Name Vibs.	Name Challenge
1938	Birth	7	11/2				
	(3)						
	(6)						
	(9)						
	(18)						
	(27)						
1968			(30)				
			2				
	(36)						
	(45)						
	(54)						
1995			(57)				
			3				
	(63)						

LIFE CYCLES INTERPRETATIONS

The following explanations for each number are divided into the Formative, Productive, and Harvest Cycles. Read the Formative Cycle number for your digit to see what your childhood and young adult life indicated; or if you are working on someone who is still a youngster, look to see what indications are included. Next, check the Productive Cycle digit and the Harvest Cycle digit for guides on what your numbers indicate. These digits vibrate from one cycle to the next, overlapping a short time into the next cycle. (As with all other number vibrations, check the keywords and number meanings in Appendix A for additional information.) Prior knowledge of each cycle's vibration could bring out the better vibrations of that cycle. When the meaning is read and understood long before it goes into effect, there is adequate time to prepare satisfactorily. Always draft the cycles and pinnacles well in advance for a successful duration.

1

Formative

This is a hard cycle for a child, because children cannot be entirely independent. So many others are in authority during the first part of life that a child usually represses the very thing that the 1 stands for. Originality, creativity, self-will, strong character, determination, intelligent interests, self-confidence, and integrity are the things a child with this number should be encouraged to develop and express. These are the vibrations of the 1 cycle. As you grow up, you must be independent and left to your own original thinking. Your originality, creativeness, and inventive mind guides you to new and individual activities. You could go into business for yourself at an early age. You would rather lead, not follow, and you can be very persistent and stubborn if you don't get your own way. You must learn to curb all egotism if you wish to keep your friends or advance in your chosen line of work.

Productive

If you are not already in business for yourself, you could possibly be the manager, or leader in some sort of way, as you have the executive ability that could push you to the top. You are independent, original, and stand on your own two feet. Dullness is not a part of your life, since new and interesting opportunities or ideas keep you on the go. Don't let your ego get the best of you. Patience and good management are a must. Your ambition, will to achieve, and inner drive should bring you success.

Harvest

People with this Harvest Cycle seldom retire, because there is always something new on the horizon challenging their ambition. This is the cycle that could bring prominent recognition into your life. In one way or another, you are at the top as leader, manager, overseer, inventor, engineer, executive, designer, or department head, positions where your leadership and originality are needed. This will always be an active cycle.

2

Formative

A child with this number could be badly spoiled and impatient, and might be raised by the mother, perhaps a divorcee or widow. The emotions are very high and tears come at any time. A 2 must learn to work with others, as this brings greatest success. Serving willingly in small ways, creating harmony, adapting to difficulty, and caring about details are just a few of the demands of this cycle. This should be a time for many friends and associates, and could mean an early marriage or partnership. Or you could have an inferiority complex and dread to meet people. You could have a musical talent or be somewhat artistic. Some 2's have psychic abilities and must be taught not to misuse them. You have the ability to get what you want without doing anything for yourself. You must be aware of the feelings of others.

Productive

This is a time for cooperation, harmony, diplomacy, and partnerships. You work well with detail. Difficulties in marriage or partnerships could appear during this cycle. Emotions run high and should be curbed. The 2's are lovers of peace and do not quarrel readily. Your manner and charm make others want to please you. You have spiritual interests and would make a good healer and comforter. You could be psychic and must use that power justly. This is a period of growth, but remember, haste makes waste. Attend to the detailed or little things. Partnerships, associations or affairs of others bring your opportunities. Cooperation and harmonious coexistence are the keys in domestic and business concerns, the keys to success. This is not the time to push yourself into the foreground, as individuality and independence are not a part of this cycle.

Harvest

This cycle will be full of friends and associates, for your ability to get along with others is important. A woman in a man's life may have great influence. This cycle usually means a restful retirement. You could be wanting to fill in a collection of some sort, such as art works, stamps, coins, dolls, special interest models, etc, as the collecting urge is strongly felt here. There should be much social activity, trips, popularity, and togetherness, because this is not a time to be alone.

3

Formative

This is the cycle to learn personal expression. Through the help and understanding of teachers and parents, this could be done through artistic and creative talents. As you get older this expression could come through writing, acting, singing, or speaking, as you should use words in as many ways as possible. Your creative abilities could lead you into some kind of designing or interior decorating. Your success comes through social or public contacts. There are many friends in this cycle. Your emotions should be kept under control, because you have a tendency to sulk if you do not get your way. Jealousy can be the 3's largest negative attitude and the hardest to overcome, and life will be very unpleasant and unhappy until it can be curbed and kept under control.

Productive

This is the cycle to be creative, original, carefree, pleasant, kind, and happy. Your original imagination should give you great inspiration and enlarge your creative talents. Now is the time for self-expression; writing, singing, lecturing, acting, or any use of words are all a possibility. You have dreams of putting some idea into positive form. In the business world this could be through literature, commercial art, designing, decorating, composing, or lecturing. Property or stocks and bonds could also hold an interest for you. You are usually an optimistic person. You are honest and sincere, and friendship means everything to you. A caution about becoming extravagant is well placed here. All in all, this should be a very pleasant cycle.

Harvest

This will be a very pleasant life with lots of friends, many activities and hobbies, and lots of social contacts. A restful period of self-expression when you can continue with your creative talents in art, music, writing, or acting. You have a way with words and should use them as often as possible. This may be the time to write that book you always wanted to write. Or is this the time to do some composing or write that play you have had in your mind for so long? Let your imagination flow into your creative mind.

4

Formative

This could be a hard life for you as a child because you will have to learn to apply yourself. School studies will be hard for you. You must learn application, practicality, management, order, and to become chore conscious early in life.

This is the time to build a good foundation for the future. Routine must be accepted and its value appreciated. All things must be practicable and serviceable. You may have to go to work early in life to earn a living, as your family may become your responsibility. You have a dream to put some idea into practical form.

Productive

This is the cycle to put all your ideas into concrete form. You are the builder, the contractor, the organizer. It is you that establishes order in all things. This could be buildings, bridges, roads, or something artistic, scientific, spiritual, or in business. This is the time to put affairs in order, to build upon that strong foundation of your life. This is the time to build that home or business but with good judgment, effort, management and order. This cycle could find you involved in large projects with lasting effects. This is a hard-working cycle, and you must be careful that you don't become a workaholic, as your health and your family relationships could suffer. In the business world you could be involved with buying and selling, education, commercial art, real estate, public utilities, employment agencies, or administration or management of any well-known company or business. Above all else, do not live in a rut. Gains are made with hard work, not laziness.

Harvest

If you were one to look ahead at this cycle, you would prepare for one in which you would be doing the work of your choice. This cycle does not forecast retirement. You will be engaged in some form of work either by necessity or by choice. You may be the boss of your own business, as the 4's prefer to give the orders, not take them. They are usually found where they have been given full charge. You attend to the smallest detail and you do not waste time or material. Be careful that you do not become "all work and no play," as this can take a toll on your health and your family. You like the quiet of the home when work is done. You have a few chosen friends with similar interests.

5

Formative

This is a cycle to learn about change and freedom. You could be restless, making sudden changes all the time, and not applying yourself to the project at hand. You are always looking for something new and exciting and never want to finish what has been started. Children under this cycle need understanding of their impulsive, hasty actions. They are the restless, the active, the curious, on-the-go type people. They need some freedom to explore, wander, delve, examine, investigate, observe, probe, study, and research. They are quick to grasp new ideas and are curious about all aspects of life. They need to be informed and guided in all aspects of sex, as the number 5 could vibrate toward the illicit side.

This cycle usually indicates many moves or changes of residence. The adolescents will be unsure, the ones who are not settled in life. They will wander from job to job looking, investigating, and searching for the proper place to work. Other numbers in their chart will give them the stability that they need. But if they have a lot of 5's, they will always show the restless side of their nature.

Productive

Because this cycle indicates constant change, you must be willing to let go of the old and useless to make way for changes, new activities, friends, jobs, residences, or travel. You will be restless and must curb your impulsive actions and decisions. There could be a change of residence in this cycle. This could be a time for promotion and progress. Your success comes away from the routine of home and regular lines of work. This could be the time for public interest, sales, advertising, stocks and bonds, and legal undertakings. You might be a travel agent, detective, secret service agent, courier, trucker, or be in occupations with variety that bring you in contact with the people. Guard against a tendency to gamble and drink. People may view you as undependable because you take your responsibilities lightly. The 5 of this cycle gives freedom to make choices. Use it wisely.

Harvest

Under this cycle a person really doesn't care if they retire or not. There could be many pleasant changes, new activities, new friends, new interests, adventure and travel. You love the strange and new. You keep in touch with world events. You are restless and impatient and often have too many irons in the fire. This is not the time to gamble or take to drink. You are bored with routine. With the 5 here you must be on the move, as change keeps you informed, entertained, educated, and away from a humdrum existence. You broaden your life by mixing with a variety of people with all kinds of educational and social backgrounds.

6

Formative

The child in this cycle will do their best to help, even at a very young age. This cycle vibrates the need to do for others. There is much duty at home. The responsibilities, obligations, home chores and duties of a child in this cycle could be lightened somewhat if the parent would lift some of the load. Their duties could include caring for a relative early in life. This is a cycle to help those in need, to learn to be useful and caring. There is love and protection through the family. A warning should be given to the young not to marry too early, as the heavy responsibilities could last through the lifetime or could lead to divorce. Your success comes through serving humankind without involving selfish interests.

Productive

Your success comes through duty and responsibility, and if accepted without personal thought, can bring financial reward and satisfaction. This is the cycle in which to serve humankind and family. You desire the beauty and perfection of your home. You are generous and charitable, sometimes to a fault. You are sympathetic, an idealist, frank, just and the peacemaker. But you may be blind to the faults of your loved ones. You prefer to work with others. You like appreciation and thanks. You can be a healer, artist, good cook or chef, gardener, singer, speaker, welfare worker, rancher, lawyer, or anything that helps others. This cycle deals with all occupations connected with the home, community, institutions, or education. This could be new, renew, or repair. You help and comfort when others are troubled. This cycle is one for marriage or divorce, as it is a period of domestic affairs. If the proper adjustments are made, this is the cycle of a happy home life.

Harvest

When you have a 6 for the Harvest Cycle it tells you to help those in need, those less fortunate than you. If you have adjusted to your duties and responsibilities, this cycle should be a very happy one. It will bring rewards or recognition for the service you have done in the past. This is not a time for lonely or useless old age, and if you are single this would be a fine time to marry. This is a time to express and receive love and affection. Enjoy art and beauty, as you like beauty in all your surroundings. This could be the time to do gardening or landscape your home. If you have retired you will enjoy the beauty of the results. If you have not adjusted to responsibilities in the past, you may find that you will be caring for family or loved ones and your retirement will be a second thought. There may be problems with children, family, marriage, divorce, home or money, but if these are faced with love and understanding they can be worked out. A 6 can be blind to the faults of loved ones. When trouble knocks on humankind's door you will always be there to help.

7

Formative

A child in this cycle usually is very misunderstood. As a child, you are quiet and contemplative, living within yourself and suffering from discrimination by those who think you are unusual. You must be encouraged to study and gain knowledge in any way possible, and strengthen the inner powers of your mind. You like to examine, explore, and question. All this is good, as it helps to fulfill your natural curiosity and inquisitive mind. Some of you will have scientific interests, others will find a special talent or delve into some unknown force of nature, some will study metaphysics. Seven is a lonely cycle, a time for books and rest. Use inside reflection and seek divine guidance. Seek nothing for personal gain or ulterior motives. Opportunities come when they are not reached for. Study, meditate, and gain knowledge.

Productive

In this cycle you do better when you work alone. Opportunities come when they are not sought after. This is a time for study, for mental development, for the scientific, the inventive. If you are interested in metaphysics, now is the time to study, to learn, to use, to write about their higher science, their law. This is the time to seek knowledge and understanding about the deeper things in life. Knowledge and skill will bring success. The 7 searches for the truth, defines the mysterious, delves into the unknown. Marriage before or after this cycle is wiser than to marry during the cycle. This cycle could find you teaching as a professor in college, sharing your vast store of knowledge with the world. Or you could be a writer of technical, scientific, or philosophical matter. You do not like physical labor or anything having to do with machinery. You do well in any occupation associated with research, analysis and study.

Harvest

You will always be searching for knowledge and wisdom. This time of life could lead to philosophical matters or research work, as you have the time to delve deeper now. This could be a cycle of semi-retirement, and you would most likely be working from your own study or lab. There will not be much activity or social life, but it will be restful, peaceful, and quiet. You will have a few chosen friends who show the same interests. This is not a cycle to marry in, because adjustments to the 7's vibrations are sometimes difficult. This cycle could also find you writing about technical matters that you have learned in the past. This is a time to study religion, whether spiritual or metaphysical.

8

Formative

Management is very important for any 8 cycle. In this cycle a child should be guided in monetary matters because misuse of money here could cause problems throughout his or her life. Eights need to be taught good judgment, sound principles, courage, effort, and ambition. You could go into business early in life, because you may be the sole supporter of your family or relatives. Misplaced trust in others could cause many problems. The best results come when working with groups, not alone. Expenses are usually high under an 8, but constant effort, good management, and a lot of ambition should pull you through.

Productive

This is the time for attainment, ambition, authority, success, and recognition. This cycle could find you managing a business or property. You want to do all things in a big way, but a caution here tells you to be careful that you do not set your goals too high, even for you. As you prefer to lead and not to follow, you are most likely in a business of your own or are the manager, supervisor, director, leader, or executive. How you manage your money can make or break you. You must learn that material things belong to all, and if they are not the most important thing in your life you should reach success. Big businesses attract you because you like to do things in a big way. You need to learn to work for personal satisfaction and not for monetary rewards, as success comes through your own efforts. The 8 is not an easy cycle but success comes through knowledge, financial effort, determination and good management. Work for outstanding results.

Harvest

When the 8 vibrates, it will always state the need for proper management or hard work, or a time to reap the benefits because it was carefully considered and carried out in the past. The vibrations of hard work and proper management of monetary or material possessions bring to this cycle the recognition of success. The person in this cycle may choose to live on those benefits and retire, or they may want to work toward semi-retirement, as they usually find themselves the owner of or in charge of a business. With proper management this cycle could increase the success and achievement of any venture, undertaking, or endeavor. An interest in clubs, organizations, and social activities brings many friendships. Expenses are always high during an 8 cycle, so careful management of money is always necessary. Problems can arise through misplaced trust in others. This would be a good time to study religion, the mystical, or philosophy.

9

Formative

This cycle can be very hard for a child to adjust to. He or she needs a large amount of understanding and love. As a child, you may feel that anything you have done goes unrecognized and unappreciated by others, and many times you become utterly confused when you are scolded when a "thank-you" and understanding should have been given. A child in this cycle often feels that he or she can do nothing right, making him or her feel nervous, sometimes frightened, unloved, and alone. This is a time to learn compassion, forgiveness, tolerance, understanding, and selfless service to humankind. One must learn that life is universal and not personal. Your success comes when the self is put behind you and the love and charity for humankind becomes your main expression. If your interests are selfish, personal, or you have resentment towards others, this cycle can be a very unhappy one. Nine is the humanitarian. You are happiest when doing for others without seeking reward. You will find that this is when reward will seek you. There could be a loss or divorce during this cycle, but it will be for the better, as the 9 always comes up with something even greater to make up for a loss.

Productive

This is the time to forget about yourself, as your success comes through unselfish service to humankind. This is not an easy number to live with unless you have learned compassion, sympathy, tolerance, understanding, and selfless service to others. If successful, this could give you the opportunity to inspire others and contribute to making a better life for all. This cycle is a time for money and fortune in business, the arts, or any line that helps humanity. Money may be made and lost and made again because this number is always a test, and if the expressions of the 9 are lived up to, much will be gained. There could be travel during this cycle also. When there is a loss in this cycle it is a way of discarding the old or unneeded to make room for something new and better needed for progress. A 9 cycle usually has a loss of some kind. Learn to let go without regret, for this was a completion that was necessary. Learn to go on and to overcome disappointments. You will have many emotional experiences during this cycle. There are constant tests of your compassion and love of others. Learn to love and to give without expecting anything in return. This is time for public life. Marriage in this cycle often is full of problems. Much can be accomplished in this cycle with a lot of effort. Legal problems come from dishonesty.

Harvest

This should be a happy time for those who understand the brotherhood of humankind. This is the time to give inspiration to the world. This may be through art work, writing a book, by setting a great example for others. This time of retirement should be one for lovers of art, beauty, drama, and philosophy. There is always time for additional learning and study in this cycle. Your interests could lead to charitable work in hospitals, institutions, service clubs, or other nonprofit organizations. If you have not learned to give and to love without expecting anything in return, this could be an unhappy time. There is usually a loss in a 9 cycle, but the 9 always gives back something better to make up for that loss. This is the time to tie up loose ends. This is the time to do great things with your talents for the benefit of all.

11

Formative

Most children under this cycle need to reduce it to the number 2 because it is too hard for them to live up to the vibrations of the 11. This is the time to bring inspiration to all through art or science. This number is considered a Master Number and stands for inspiration, revelation, knowledge, and leadership along spiritual lines. You are an idealist and could become a teacher, philosopher, or psychologist. High personal ambitions could be a downfall. You belong before the public and like the limelight. You could have psychic abilities.

Productive

This is a time for spiritual expansion, not a time for getting involved with the business world. You have an inner force that helps you bring knowledge and inspiration to humanity. We often find artists, scientists, teachers, writers, explorers, charity workers, reformers, psychics, inventors, ministers, and leaders in this cycle. There is a warning here against high personal ambitions; it could be your downfall. This number could also represent the hands of a healer, physician, or peacemaker. This could be a cycle of much nervous tension. Also check the interpretation under Productive Cycle number 2. Many do not vibrate to the hard limitations of the 11.

Harvest

This retirement period may find you writing about the mystical or spiritual things of life. You have the time now to do the reading and researching that you want to do to expand your mind. You may find yourself in the limelight and in demand because of the knowledge that you obtain. You can be an inspiration to others. This is a time for the spiritual, not the material. When the 11 vibrates here, it wants to say, "The world needs me." Also look to the Harvest Cycle number 2 for those who do not vibrate with the 11.

22

Formative

There isn't a 22nd month, so there isn't a 22 Formative Cycle. A Formative 22 would be impossible to live up to.

Productive

This is the time for big ideas, huge achievements, and top leadership, the cycle for the master builder, engineer, architect, or other expansive thinker. It is time for large groups of people, or helping the world through diplomatic service. A time for large cooperative interests, international concerns, or world affairs. A time to assume leadership, to manage or direct. A time to follow your hunches. You should be doing work before or for the public. Your views should be universal, not personal, as you must contribute to the general welfare of all humankind. It is a time to combine materialism and idealism. Nerves and emotions are a hazard. Try to keep them under control. Like the vibrations of the 11, this Master Number may be too strong for some, so look to the 4 Productive Cycle for direction.

Harvest

Because of the activity involved with this number you may not retire. You have a high nervous energy that keeps you on the go. This cycle could find you directing or managing a large concern, or as a diplomat, ambassador, or public benefactor. Or are you a professor or teacher in a college or university? This is the time to do big things for all humankind. Now is the time to write that book. There are many large activities vibrating during this cycle. When the 22 is not capable of defining the way someone feels or lives life, always check the single digit of the 4. Here too, the Harvest Cycle of the 4 may be the correct vibration for those finding this one too hard to live up to.

Birth Day Vibrations

The next three birth day vibrations use the *day* only of the birth date. This birthday vibration number is the same number as the Productive Cycle digit, so it will have many of the same vibrations. If need be, reduce this number to a single digit. The higher the number, the higher the intensity of the vibrations.

Example: Day of Birth: 20 = 2 + 0 = 2 Birth Day Vibration.

BIRTH DAY VIBRATION INTERPRETATIONS

The calendar day of birth indicates the hidden, inner talent that could be applied in the selection of careers and other important decisions.

THE 1 NUMBERS (birth day on the 1st, 10th, 19th or 28th)
 You will have the mental and individual vibrations of the 1.
  1st Independent, original, creative, natural leader, pioneer.
  10th Creative, artistic, idealistic, not domestically inclined.
  19th All of the above. Subject to extremes, highs and lows.
  28th Affectionate, daydreamer, independent, strong-willed.

THE 2 NUMBERS (birth day on the 2nd, 11th, 20th, or 29th)
 You will have a dual nature, being able to see both sides. Peacemaker, follower.
  2nd Sensitive, emotional, work better in groups, may be doormat.
  11th Master Number. Inspirational, psychic, highly emotional.
  20th Tactful, diplomatic, musical, higher 2 octave.
  29th Extremist, dreamer, need home background (2 + 9 see the 11th).

THE 3 NUMBERS (birth day on the 3rd, 12th, 21st, or 30th)
 Your life will be pleasant. You have a gift with words and are creative.
  3rd Friend, artistic, self-expression, intellectual, humorous.
  12th Practical, disciplinarian, designer, good reasoning power.

21st Socially inclined, entertainer, nervous, many interests.
30th Actor, imaginative, intuitive, dislike hard work (higher 3).

THE 4 NUMBERS (birth day on the 4th, 13th, 22nd, or 31st)
You are dependable and practical—the builders and workers.
4th Orderly, honest, good at detail, stubborn, hidden affections.
13th Manager, hard worker, need home background (see the 4th).
22nd Master Number. Universalist, intuitive, emotional, nervous.
31st Good business ability, need responsibility, loyal, determined.

THE 5 NUMBERS (birth day on the 5th, 14th, or 23rd)
You desire freedom and change. Willing to try anything new.
5th Follow hunches, versatile, investigative, intellectual.
14th Dual natured, sympathetic, lucky at gambling, emotional.
23rd Professional, healer, quick thinker, good personality.

THE 6 NUMBERS (birth day on the 6th, 15th, or 24th)
You crave love, friends, companionship. Assume responsibilities.
6th Love home and community, musical, devoted parent, stubborn.
15th Attracts opportunities, learn by doing, artistic, generous.
24th Family person, care of elderly, civic work, solid citizen.

THE 7 NUMBERS (birth day on the 7th, 16th, or 25th)
You crave knowledge. Intellectual, scientific, loner. Dislike manual labor.
7th Perfectionist, psychic, individualist, keen mind, stubborn.
16th Analytical, moody, wants affection, need world contacts.
25th Intuitive, interested in metaphysics, underestimate self.

THE 8 NUMBERS (birth day on the 8th, 17th, or 26th)
You are mentally well-balanced. Manage in the business world.
8th Executive ability, money maker, good judge of values.
17th Good business sense, set in your ways, materially inclined.
26th Good organizer, emotional, proud of family and home.

THE 9 NUMBERS (birth day on the 9th, 18th, or 27th)
You are the big brother to humanity. Compassionate, selfless service.
9th Humanitarian, artistic, intellectual, philanthropist, generous.
18th Independent, efficient, adviser, must learn to live for others.
27th Versatile, forceful, determined, psychic, emotional, nervous.

CHALLENGES OF BIRTH DAY

Using the birth day number again, this is a lesson to be learned. Its vibration could cause anxiety or tension in life until it is overcome or learned. Subtract the smallest number from the largest for all double number days and 0 from all single-numbered days. The 11 and 22, being Master Numbers, have a challenge of 0, which is different from having no challenge. Because these two numbers are accompanied by gifts of inspiration and revelation, they are given all the challenges rolled into one. No particular challenge is going to give them any big problems. All Birth Day Challenges will be felt during the whole life but will have the strongest vibrations during the Productive Cycle. You will learn about other Challenges farther into this book.

Example: Day of Birth: 20 = 2 − 0 = 2 Birth Day Challenge.

Fill in the work area below with the day that you are using.

Day of Birth _____ = ____ − ____ = _____ Birth Day Challenge.

BIRTH DAY CHALLENGE INTERPRETATIONS

The lower the number of a Challenge, the higher its potency will be, which is just the opposite of positive numbers.

Challenge of **0** Small amount of all vibrations in one.
Challenge of **1** Become independent.
Challenge of **2** Gain self-confidence.
Challenge of **3** Learn self-expression.
Challenge of **4** Be dependable, not lazy.
Challenge of **5** Accept and develop change.
Challenge of **6** Acknowledge obligations.
Challenge of **7** Learn faith not fear.
Challenge of **8** Learn sense of values.
Challenge of **9** Learn compassion.

BIRTH DAY GIFT

This is a gift given to offset the Birth Day Challenge. Subtract the Challenge from the ultimate number of nine to find the Birthday Gift number.

Example:

The Ultimate Number	9
Subtract the Birth Day Challenge digit	−2
The Birthday Gift number:	7

Fill in the work area below with the data that you are using.

The Ultimate Number	9
Subtract the Birth Day Challenge digit	− ___
The Birthday Gift number:	

Transfer these digits to the worksheet. See the sample below for our George.

Birth Day Vibrations	2
Day Challenges	2
Day Gift	7

BIRTH DAY GIFT INTERPRETATIONS

IF: The Challenge is **0** (9 − 0 = 9)   the Gift is **9** · Compassion
The Challenge is **1** (9 − 1 = 8)   the Gift is **8** · Achievement
The Challenge is **2** (9 − 2 = 7)   the Gift is **7** · Wisdom
The Challenge is **3** (9 − 3 = 6)   the Gift is **6** · Accomplishment
The Challenge is **4** (9 − 4 = 5)   the Gift is **5** · Steadfastness
The Challenge is **5** (9 − 5 = 4)   the Gift is **4** · Patience
The Challenge is **6** (9 − 6 = 3)   the Gift is **3** · Originality
The Challenge is **7** (9 − 7 = 2)   the Gift is **2** · Understanding
The Challenge is **8** (9 − 8 = 1)   the Gift is **1** · Ambition
The Challenge is **9** (9 − 9 = 0)   the Gift is **0** · Knowledge

The 9 will need all gifts to make up for its hard challenge, so knowledge (to be used wisely) is their award.

Attainments (Pinnacles)

The Attainments, or Pinnacles, are a way of reading the high points or coming events in our lives. They can foretell what type of experience we could meet in our travels down the Path of Life. They can help us to look ahead and know just what we must develop to make life easier. We can look back at past Attainments to see into which direction life was pointing us. Knowledge will help us reach the height of the Attainment.

There are four distinct Attainment cycles in life. Each represents the high point that may be reached during the vibration period of that Attainment's digit. They signify mild or serious changes and have a genuine influence on life. A helping hand is given if a digit agrees with or matches the Path of Life or one of its sub-paths, the Soul Urge, The Expression digit, or the Reality Number (the last three will be taught later). The helping hand, or stronger vibration, is working only when that particular Attainment cycle is operating and could intensify the vibrations to a higher level, giving the push that is needed to succeed.

A positive life leads to happiness and life's goals, but negative attitudes can lead one to unhappiness and a life of hardships. Attainments are fixed sub-paths of life and greatly affect the Path of Life one way or another. In a few cases the power of an Attainment may be vibrating stronger than the Path of Life. Second and third periods are very important, with greater emphasis placed on the third, where the planning of the balance of life should be done. All the higher numeric vibrations are harder for a child and easier for an adult.

FORMULA FOR THE LENGTH OF THE ATTAINMENTS

Because numerology cycles in numbers from 1 through 9, the base number is 9. There are four Attainments, so we will use a formula of $9 \times 4 = 36$. To find the age each Attainment Cycle ends, or the duration of each cycle, start with the number 36 and subtract the Path of Life digit. This gives you the age when the FIRST ATTAINMENT Cycle ends, and being the longest cycle it runs from birth to that age. The SECOND ATTAINMENT starts there and operates through the next nine years, so add nine years to the age of the the First Attainment Cycle to find the end of that cycle. The THIRD ATTAINMENT runs through the next nine years, so add nine more years to the age of the Second Attainment Cycle. The FOURTH ATTAINMENT runs through the remainder of life. Attainments take effect on the birthday, with maximum effects vibrating in a 1 Personal Year.

You will see just how easy it is to find these durations when you fill in the blanks below with your numbers. Our examples are to the right.

			(Our example)
(always use number 36 here)	36		36
Subtract Path of Life	− __		− 7
1st Attainment ends at age		(and Second begins)	29
Add 9 more years	+ 9		+ 9
2nd Attainment ends at age		(and Third begins)	38
Add 9 more years	+ 9		+ 9
3rd Attainment ends at age		(and Fourth begins)	47

The Fourth Attainment runs for the rest of life.

FINDING THE ATTAINMENT DIGITS

We just figured the duration of the Attainments. Now let's find the actual digit that will be vibrating in each duration. Remember to reduce each one to a single digit only.

We will be using the birth month, birth day, and the year digits again. Using your numbers and the examples below as a guide, fill in your work areas. (Attainments are considered as *positive* vibrations, so always *ADD* when using their digits in the workbook.)

1. FIRST ATTAINMENT: (The *month* of birth digit plus the *day* of birth digit)

Example: Month   2
         Add Day + 2
         Equals   4

Month of Birth Digit

Add Day of Birth Digit + __

Reduce if needed   = __ + __ = ____ **1st Attainment**

2. SECOND ATTAINMENT: (*day* of birth digit plus the *year* of birth digit)
   Example: Day   2
                   Add Year +3__
                   Equals   5

   Day of Birth Digit

   Add Year of Birth Digit +___

   Reduce to single digit   = __ + __ = ____ **2nd Attainment**

3. THIRD ATTAINMENT: (The total of the First and Second Attainments)
   Example: Sum of 1. above   4
            Add sum of 2. above +5__
                   Equals   9

   Digit of First Attainment

   Add Digit of 2nd Attainment +___

   Reduce to single digit   = __ + __ = ____ **3rd Attainment**

4. FOURTH ATTAINMENT: (The birth *month* plus the of birth *year* digit)
   Example: Month   2
                Add Year   +3__
                Equals   5

   Month of Birth Digit

   Add Year of Birth Digit   +___

   Reduce if needed   = __ + __ = ____ **4th Attainment**

Using George's example on the next page and the worksheet in the front of this book, you can place these digits and their years in the proper places on your worksheet. Figure the year that corresponds with each Attainment age and place them in the year column. Be sure to match the year with the age. If any of the year numbers are the same as a cycle number year, just draw your line in the proper column across from that same year. You would not rewrite a duplicate year number.

Like the Life Cycles, I put the age of the start of the Attainments in parentheses (29) above the line of the Attainment digits. This makes it easier to check the chart at a glance, since the answers will already be there and you won't need to refigure.

Year	(Age)	Path of Life	Life Cycles	Attainments or Pinnacles	Life's Challenges	Name Vibs.	Name Challenge
1938	Birth	7		4			
	(3)						
	(6)						
	(9)						
	(18)						
	(27)						
1967				(29)			
				5			
	(36)						
1976				(38)			
				9			
	(45)						
1985				(47)			
				5			

ATTAINMENTS/PINNACLES INTERPRETATIONS

The Attainments listed here give a small portion of the many meanings for each number. We advise you to read into each number the keywords or the numeric value meanings if you do not find the exact project or activity that fits your life. The meanings of each number hold the same vibrations listed in different places, and using your interpretation you should check all to see what fits your need for the path you are taking in this life.

1

A time to individualize. Action, change. A time to stand on your own two feet. A time for independence. A time of new beginnings. A time to think and act for yourself. It could be a hard pinnacle for the young, because they may not be ready to stand up to life or be able to handle the requirements of leadership or self-government. This is the time for originality, imagination, invention, or creativity. A time to push your own special talent to the front. A time to pioneer in a field you may have kept in the background. A time to lead, manage, conduct, guide, or pilot. Make use of your personal ideas. When this Attainment matches another important number vibrating, it makes it stronger, more active.

2

Cooperation, patience, consideration of others, sharing—the diplomat, arbitrator, or peacemaker. You work better in partnerships and groups. This is not a time to do things alone, because 2's need companionship to function at their best. This could be a time of great emotion. Tears could flow at the drop of a hat. Try to overcome this sensitiveness. Because the 2's work so well with others, they make our great ambassadors and diplomats. They also work well in business and public affairs. This period could be a time for disharmony in partnerships or marriage. It could bring about a dissolution. Be aware of the feelings of others. The 2 means to help others who are in need, or it could mean for you to accept the help offered if you are in need.

3

This pleasant time in life could be used for the creative, the inspirational, the artistic, or the personal expression in all you do. This is a mental, not a physical pinnacle. A time to channel your talents into some specific creative calling. This could be writing, singing, acting, or speaking, as 3's have a way with words. This is a time to enjoy being with people—3's have many friends. Enjoy the pleasures of life. The 3 will always vibrate the artistic talents wanting to come out.

4

Management and order vibrate here. This number will always be hard for the young, but it teaches good working habits. Many go to work early in life. The family may be a heavy responsibility. Now is the time to establish a solid foundation, to be practical, to arrange and organize. This could be a period of constant, hard work. A time to save and accumulate for the future. This could be a time to put your constructive ideas to practical use. A time to construct, strive, and systemize to accomplish gratifying results.

5

Many new experiences, changes, activities. New friends, new places, new jobs. Restlessness, constant travel, freedom to come and go, possibly a change in residence. This could be a time for promotion and progress. You must be willing to let go of the old to make way for the new changes that come here. Try to avoid impulsive actions and decisions. It is best to keep a few roots down, but your success comes away from the routine of home and regular work lines. You do not like being in a rut. Freedom could be too big to handle in a first cycle, causing some to make serious mistakes concerning the use of their senses; sex in particular could be a problem. In the last cycle it could mean lots of travel and variety, and you possibly will not retire. In any of the cycles it could mean public interest, sales, advertising, travel agents, matters of foreign interest, legal undertakings, or stocks and bonds.

6

Obligations to the duties of home, family, love, and other burdens. You may have the responsibilities of a relative. You may be serving humankind, because the success of the 6 comes through service to others without personal or selfish interests involved. If a positive attitude is vibrating, this could be a period of success, love, romance, marriage, and financial security. If negative vibrations are shown, this could be a time for divorce, friction, and other conflicts. This is the best cycle for marriage, but the very young should be careful about early marriage, since it could give them a long life of responsibility and duty. A 6 in early life could mean a lot of home duties. On the other cycles it should mean a happy home life. Happiness and success comes from helping others. This is not the time to be selfish.

7

Knowledge, philosophy, analysis, religion, seclusion, and understanding the unknown in life. Your interests lie in the educational, scientific, the spiritual, or the metaphysical. Your knowledge and skill brings success. Usually by choice this is a time of loneliness; but if you use it for study, meditation, or introspection you will be so involved you won't really notice and you will become much wiser. It is advisable to marry before or after this pinnacle. As children, 7's are usually misunderstood, for others think that because he or she lives within him/herself, he/she must be unusual. If they are encouraged to study and left to think their own thoughts, they could surprise all with their super intelligence. Last cycle 7's could lead to some kind of research or philosophical work. This is the time to inquire and delve deeper into the mysteries of life.

8

Accomplishment, ambition, authority, success, recognition. An 8 is usually in charge of or a manager of business or property. On a first cycle, 8's should be guided in monetary matters, or they could misuse money throughout their life. They may go into business early in life. All 8 pinnacles could mean material gain if it is worked for through good judgment, sound principles, proper management, courage, and with lots of ambition and drive. This is not a time to be lazy, selfish, or extravagant. This is not a time to rely on luck. Expenses are usually high during this period, so good management and budgeting are a must. Disappointments could come because of bad judgment and misplaced trust in people. Work for big results.

9

Compassion, tolerance, impersonality, sympathy, selflessness, completion, and a universal outlook are the vibrations of this digit. This pinnacle is essentially for the love of humankind, shown by practical kindness and helpfulness to others. You are the big brother to all. A selfish life will not be tolerated under this number. The difficult part of this number is that you must learn to be a humanitarian without expecting any return. A divorce or unhappy love affair may take place in a First Attainment, but remember that this can be fortunate, because a 9 always brings something better in return. This is a hard pinnacle for a child, for they feel alone, nervous, and sometimes terrified. They may not receive the love or appreciation that they were expecting. This is hard for a child to understand. A 9 could be a period of huge success in business, art, or philanthropic lines of work. Life would be well rewarded if you live up to the expressions of the 9. Later Attainments are the time to do great things with your talents for the benefit of all.

11

Inspiration, spiritual expansion, the mystical side of life. This pinnacle may be too hard for a child, and most often should be reduced to a 2. You have the opportunity to work, teach, or inspire along artistic, emotional, or other motivational lines. This is not a time for anything in the commercial world. You are high strung or nervous, yet you can appear calm, cool, and collected. You are highly emotional. This pinnacle gives you the opportunity to be in the limelight. You may become inventive or show religious tendencies. The 11 has the psychic powers to know the difference between worldly and spiritual deeds. They need to give to be happy. Read the 2 Attainment, for you may find this number too hard to live up to, and the 2 could better fit the vibrations needed here.

22

This Master Number vibrates to the Universe. It wants the world to know that those special enough to live up to its vibration are concerned enough to do all in their power to help humankind. Large cooperative interests, international concerns, and world affairs are all a part of the 22's vibrations. Huge accomplishments can be made under this pinnacle. Assume leadership, manage and direct. This is the time for building big things for the benefit of the world. Your views should be universal, not personal. You should follow your hunches. You should be doing work before the public and in large groups, because you must contribute to the general welfare of all humankind. This Attainment may be hard for some to live up to, so check the number 4 to see if that vibration is better suited here.

Life's Challenges
(Attainment Challenges)

There are one Major and two Minor Challenges (some have an additional Minor Challenge) affecting the Path of Life, the Life Cycles, and Attainments or Pinnacles. They are like pebbles, rocks, or boulders in your way down life's road. Their size is determined by the vibration of the Challenge number. You must learn how to remove these obstacles as you continue on your way. A clear, smooth road hinges on overcoming and applying these lessons to life, thus setting the rocks aside where they remain as a reminder or marker that they could roll back again if forgotten.

We are given more understanding because of the experiences we have in overcoming a Challenge. Challenges should be considered as incentives. They are the lessons in life to be learned, and learn them we must, or their vibrations will not let us advance along life's path without many false starts, stumbles, and falls. The sooner we meet a Challenge and learn its lesson, the sooner will that challenge be smoothed out and its vibrations weakened.

FORMULA

Challenges are negative vibrations or something lacking, a minus in your life, so you always SUBTRACT when working with their digits. *The smaller digit is always subtracted from the larger digit,* regardless of where they are placed. Life's Challenges use the digits of the month of birth, day of birth, and the year of birth. Follow the examples (for November 20, 1938) below as a guide to fill in your work areas.

1st Minor Challenge example:

Month	2
Birth Day	−2
Equals	0

Birth Month Digit

Subtract Birth Day Digit −_____

= **1st Minor Challenge**
(vibrates most during first half of life)

2nd Minor Challenge example:

Birth Day	2
Birth Year	-3
Equals	1

Birth Day Digit

Subtract Birth Year Digit $-$ ___

(Subtract lesser from greater)   = **2nd Minor Challenge**

(vibrates most during last half of life)

Major Challenge example:

Subtract 1st Minor Challenge digit	0
from the 2nd Minor Challenge digit	-1
Equals	1

1st Minor Challenge Digit

Subtract 2nd Minor Challenge Digit $-$ ___

= **Major Challenge**

(felt throughout life)

ADDITIONAL CHALLENGE

A small number of people have a 4th Challenge. This Challenge, which acts as an *additional* Minor Challenge, will be a casual influence throughout life. Figure it by using the following formula:

The month of birth digit is subtracted from the year of birth digit (lesser from greater). If the number reached matches any of the other three Challenges, there is no additional Challenge. If a new number shows, it indicates that the life has an additional Challenge and an *extra* obstacle to conquer.

Birth Month Digit

Subtract Birth Year Digit $-$ ___

= **Additional Minor Challenge**

LIFE'S CHALLENGES INTERPRETATIONS

The Challenges that we worked with here are called Life's Challenges because their effects are felt upon the Path of Life, Life Cycles, and the Attainments. They are all found by using only the numbers in the birth date.

These lessons or obstacles in life run from numbers 0 through 8. There cannot be a 9 Challenge here. (There are 9's listed in the Birth Day and Ruling Passion Challenges.) The 0 Challenge is ALL Challenges rolled up into one with small vibrations from each. Use special care when translating any of these Challenge digits if they match a Path of Life, Life Cycle, or Attainment digit, so that the negative vibrations of the Challenge do not overpower the positive vibrations of that specific path. The Major Challenge represents the strongest vibration all through life, while the 1st Minor vibrates mostly in the first half of life, and the 2nd in the last.

The same general meanings are used for all Challenges in numerology regardless of where they are located. You will be taught how to find additional Challenges in the name section, in Personal vibrations from the present year, month, or day, and in other sections of this workbook.

Using the worksheet at the front of the book, place all of your Challenge digits in their proper places on the line titled Life's Challenges and in the chart under the Life's Challenges column. Use George's chart at the front of the book as an example.

0

The 0 Challenge is really giving *you* the choice of its challenge. If your life is filled with positive vibrations, you do not have any specific challenge. To have reached this point you must have overcome all the other Challenges combined and learned their lessons in another time and another place. If your life has negative vibrations you will find that this Challenge can give you all the other Challenges rolled up into one. They may only be subtle challenges, but if your negative vibrations are very strong, they could make themselves very well known to you. The main thing to remember about the 0 Challenge is that you are making the choice as to how it will affect your life.

1

The Me Firster. The ego is one of the strongest challenges of the 1. You try to get others to do your bidding. To correct this attitude you must stop thinking that the world is yours and that everyone in it must do as you desire.This challenge can also represent someone who is being held back, their individuality kept in control by someone else, usually a relative. Encouraging inner drive and standing on one's own two feet is the way to overcome this. The challenge of the 1 is to learn to individualize, become independent, and get ambitious. Overcome stubbornness, impatience, arrogance, selfishness, and laziness.

2

Cooperation, working with people. You need to develop confidence in yourself. You let your emotions get in the way. This may cause an inferiority complex, which leaves the way open for others to walk all over you. You must learn to work with others. This does not mean being a doormat. You have ideas of your own too, and these can be used in conjunction with the ideas of others to benefit all. Two heads are better than one. Overcome shyness, carelessness regarding detail, lack of consideration for others, unwillingness to cooperate, and blindly following as others lead.

3

The need for self-expression. You are unsure of yourself and prefer to stay in the background. This could be due to an aversion to personal criticism. Don't let others hold you back. You have the talents needed to express yourself in any way you wish. This could be through speech, writing, or an artistic talent. Just be careful that you are not the one speaking impulsively, hurting others with your words, because this could bring you a great loss of popularity, admiration, friends, and romance. Get out into the world and dance, sing, play, speak, or write. Express yourself. Rid yourself of that inferiority complex. Avoid extravagant clothing and ornamentation. Do not gossip.

4

This is a dual challenge pertaining to work. It could go either way. Are you lazy, impatient, shiftless, undependable, unsteady, or unobservant? Or are you a workaholic, in a rut, a perfectionist, a stickler for detail? To overcome this challenge you must realize that there is work to be done, a foundation to be laid. Procrastination must be overcome and your orderly, practical side brought to the surface. If you are a workaholic, remember that "all work and no play," etc. is your motto. Too much work could be harmful to your health. Four's should not be too opinionated.

5

You have a fear of change. You must learn to accept and develop change. You like to hang on to things and to people that need to be let go. You must learn when to change and what to change. This challenge can also represent a desire to escape from responsibilities. If so, you have such a deep personal need for freedom that it makes you resentful and impatient. You want to try everything at least once and are curious about pleasures that involve the senses. This challenge could make you very impulsive toward pleasures of the self. To overcome this challenge you must welcome and take advantage of new situations. Learn to adapt. Do a variety of things but try to finish each one. Don't stay in a rut. Keep a sound and healthy curiosity about life. You must get over your fear of new places, people, and things.

6

This challenge deals with the home and marriage, domestic responsibility, and service to others. It could show that you have an unwillingness to accept the responsibilities needed here, or it could be a challenge of one who is overbearing. Do you demand that others do your bidding? Are you domineering and interfering? You must learn to accept things and people as they are. You must realize that people have a right to be what they want to be and to have their own opinions. There is a service to humankind to be learned here. Learn to teach others, to heal them, but do so without the determination to remake them in your own image. If someone does not agree with you, don't argue with them. Learn to accept your responsibilities and don't be a busybody; make life as harmonious as possible and learn to give advice only when it is asked for. Keep your surroundings beautiful. Your motto could be "live and let live." Don't be smug, self-opinionated and self-righteous, and remember that you, too, can be wrong sometimes.

7

This is the challenge of the misunderstood. You impress others as being aloof, lazy, moody, silent, and glum. You live your own inner life, giving you a feeling of withdrawal from the world. You must learn to be alone and not lonely. You must always be in search of knowledge. You must learn to study, to question, to pry, to answer. You must bring yourself out of the background and share your knowledge with the world, but without gloating about what you know or how you obtained your knowledge. Don't dwell on your limitations—have faith, not fear. You must develop patience and understanding. If you remain aloof, you will not find happiness in human relationships. The curse of drink could be a challenge. Remember that the challenges of the 7 are self-imposed.

8

Irresponsibility. This challenge shows a false sense of values. You will learn that if you depend too much on material things, whether money or assets, you will lose them. The challenge will be a lesson showing you that the material things belong to everyone; and as you learn to take things as they come and not to expect the best, the most, or all, you will be given these things. You will need to learn how to handle money, because if you do not manage it properly, you could lose it. The challenge of the 8 shows recklessness, abuse of power, and lack of detail. You must develop efficiency and management. Cultivate broader outlooks and suppress limitations. This challenge could also mean a complete disregard for material things, leading to wastefulness becoming as destructive as miserliness. If the 0 is the *first* sub-challenge for the 8, it means a self-made person. If the 8 is the first sub-challenge, one is in danger of becoming mercenary. The 8 as a *final* challenge warns us of a loss of material things if our priorities are not kept in order.

Health Indications

Some numerologists use all numbers as health indicators. They look at the whole chart to find the numbers that appear often and in large quantities. These are the numbers they use to indicate health precautions or to designate where symptoms could occur.

Some numerologists use just the Challenges and the numbers making up the Challenges as an indication of some kind of medical problem in that area. They also look at any number that matches any of the major numbers in the chart.

The numbers below are assigned to parts of the body.

0   Like the 0 Challenge, this 0 could indicate any or all parts of the body.

1   Head, headaches, eyes, nose, mouth, teeth.

2   Any part needed for speech—throat, tongue, neck.

3   Sympathetic nervous system, nervous indigestion, migraines, ulcers, solar plexus, spleen (white blood cells).

4   Lungs, stomach, liver, gall bladder, skin.

5   Heart, blood, circulation.

6   Chronic conditions.

7   Kidneys.

8   Reproductive organs, colon.

9   Feet, all other areas, and diseases hard to control.

Universal Vibrations
(Year, Month, Day, Hour)

These are the vibrations in which our world operates. Before the world was formed, all that the Universe had were numbers. When the world was formed it was set in motion by the vibrations of the Universe. These are the vibrations used for worldly things such as national or international business, government projects, or local affairs—nonpersonal matters.

A Universal Year digit is needed to find the vibrations for worldwide enterprises. This digit is also needed to figure a Universal Month digit, which in turn is used to find a Universal Day digit.

A Universal Year digit is also needed to find the digit for a Personal Year, which is needed to find the Personal Month, Personal Day, and Personal Hour. So we must know how to figure the Universal Year first.

The Universal Year runs its cycle from January 1st through December 31st. The same is true with the Personal Year. They are computed this way because it is the Universal Year digit or Personal Year digit that has the influence on the person, place or thing, *not* the person giving the influence to the date. These digits always change on January 1st of a new year because that is when the numbers or digits change for that year. Please pay special attention to this duration.

UNIVERSAL YEAR

To find a Universal Year you reduce the four numbers of the year in question to a single digit. Use the year numbers only, not the month or day.

Enter the YEAR you are using _____. Reduce to a single digit.

1 + 9 + __ + __ = ____ = __ + __ = __ U.Y. (UNIVERSAL YEAR)

UNIVERSAL YEAR INTERPRETATIONS

The following descriptions for the Universal Years are only a small part of the vibrations of each number, which has effects worldwide. These are just to give you an idea of what each Universal Year could be. The general meanings of each number could apply in a broad sense for any Universal Year in question (see Appendix A).

1

New beginnings. Much activity. The pioneering spirit makes way for new inventions, new discoveries, or new creations.

2

Peace treaties. Arbitrations. Agreements between nations. Ambassadors or diplomats in peaceful, political discussions.

3

A pleasant social time involving theaters, sports, or any kind of amusement or entertainment. The year of the arts, the antiques, or shows that display museum pieces or other collectables.

4

This is the time to build firm, worldly foundations for lasting success. A year of hard work. Economy and good management are necessary.

5

Worldwide changes. Variety, activity, new interests, new jobs. Worldwide interest in metaphysics.

6

A year for developing public parks and recreational facilities. The building of new houses and buildings for community or civic affairs. Responsibilities and concerns turn to worldly matters.

7

The year for mental activities, with the world or the Universe in mind. This is the year to invent for the benefit of all. The world sees more interest in spiritual and mystical things.

8

Acceleration and advancement in big business ventures. Achievements. Foreign exchange. Large engineering feats. Good management brings prosperity.

9

Help and understanding of humankind. The tying up of loose ends. The old moves out, making way for the new. Completions and eliminations make way for next year and an all-new 9-year cycle to start again.

11

Worldwide interest increases in spirituality, religion, and metaphysics. Inventions, inspirations, and idealism are extensive. The next one will be 2009.

22

The year for the master builders of the world. Big businesses or expansions that are concrete, visible and tangible, constructed with the whole human race in mind.

UNIVERSAL MONTH

The Universal Month vibration is for local, county, state, city, country or world matters (anything nonpersonal), and it has its own digit action. To find a Universal Month, add the digit of the calendar month to the Universal Year digit and reduce, if need be, to a single digit.

Write in the MONTH you are using _____ . Reduce to single digit.

    U.Y. Digit

  Month digit   +___

      Total   = __ + __ = _____ U.M. (UNIVERSAL MONTH)

UNIVERSAL MONTH INTERPRETATIONS

The following are only a few of the vibrations for a Universal Month.

1

Originality, new ideas. New leaders (committees, board chairperson, etc).

2

World peace, cooperation between nations, a time to collect statistics, national and political matters.

3

Creativity or inventions for worldwide use. Worldwide entertainment by singers, actors, or lecturers.

4

Hard, detailed work, skill and exactness, solid foundations made for national or international projects.

5

Worldwide changes and action. The unusual and unexpected. Much travel for business, sales, or speculation.

6

The time to beautify and clean up the environment, build parks, handle civic affairs, initiate humanitarian projects.

7

A month to study, plan, search, invent, or analyze something needed by the world.

8

This month brings organization to business or corporate enterprises on a large scale.

9

A month for completion or elimination of the necessary to make way for the next month's new. Concern for humanity.

11

Spiritual activity, inspiration, metaphysics.

22

Large construction or improvements to national and international enterprises.

UNIVERSAL DAY

Each Universal Day has its own 24-hour vibration of a nonpersonal nature. The Universal Day is found by adding the day of the month to the Universal Month digit and, if need be, reducing that total to a single digit.

Write in the DAY you are using _____. Reduce to single digit.

U.M. Digit

Day Digit +___

Total   = __ + __ = ____ U.D. (UNIVERSAL DAY)

UNIVERSAL DAY INTERPRETATIONS

The following are a few of the influences that could be felt on a Universal Day.

1

This day could bring new ideas, new beginnings, or new additions to things done for the surrounding area. Its wide implications could include cities, towns, states, etc.

2

This Universal Day needs the cooperation of others to put plans together for the benefit of all.

3

A 3 means creation on a large scale in all areas. It means inventions, art displays, or designs for the public.

4

This 4 means the surrounding area can benefit from the management or order needed to make things work.

5

This is the time to make changes in plans or add changes to make plans work for public ventures.

6

A time to beautify surrounding areas. Landscaping, flower gardens, and parks are all a part of this vibration.

7

The 7 tells the world it is time to rest, relax, read, study, or investigate.

8

Build on a larger scale; manage, organize, or expand for success and accomplishment. All planning committees need vibrations from this number.

9

Time to put the finishing touches on most projects. Humanitarian needs fit this vibration.

11

A day for contemplation and retrospection, for science, religion and the mysteries of life (see number 2).

22

The master plans. Build in a big way for all. Big plans, big jobs, big improvements (see number 4).

Personal Vibrations
(Year, Month, Day, Hour)

These are vibrations affecting you personally. We all have our own Personal vibrations each year, month, day, and hour. In the same Universal Year, a person with a certain Personal number will receive vibrations that are different from the vibrations felt by a person with another Personal number. Many people will have the same Personal number vibrating for them at the same time, but each person may use it or interpret it in a different way.

PERSONAL YEAR

The Personal Year digit is the most powerful of the Personal vibrations. The next strongest is the Personal Month, followed by the Personal Day and Hour respectively. Each 1 to 9 year will have its own vibration which cannot be evaded. The vibrations are there whether you know, feel, or recognize it. You can take advantage of the major ones and curb some of the setbacks by knowing when these will occur. The fullest meaning of the Personal Year is sensed during a 1 Personal Month.

The Personal Years run in a nine-year cycle, beginning with each 1 Personal Year and continuing on for the next nine years. Vibrations are the most intense from January 1st to September 30th, when the next year's vibration starts edging in. The first three months of the new year could have leftover vibrations from unfinished matters of the past year.

Your Path of Life is the Personal Year digit for the year you were born. This digit starts you on your own cycle wherever that digit is. Our George started his cycle in a 7 Personal Year, and on January 1, 1939 he went into an 8 Personal Year. As with all other numbers, if any Personal digit matches a major Path or sub-path there could be stronger vibrations and helping hands.

As you learned in the Life Cycles section, to figure a Personal Year you need the birth month, the day of birth and the Universal Year number for the date in question.

Example for George:

Birth Month — Nov.	11 =	2
Day of Birth — 20th	20 =	2
Universal Year — 1984	1984 =	22
Totals	2015 =	26 = 8 P.Y.

Now you try it.

```
                Month of Birth

                Day of Birth

                Universal Year  +__

                Total. Reduce.        = __ + __ + __ + __ = ___ =

                                        __ + __ = ___ P.Y.
```

A quicker way to figure a Personal Year is to add the single digits.

Birth Digit (B.D.)	(Birth Month + Birth Day)
Plus U.Y. Digit +__	(from your Universal work area)
Total. Reduce. = __ + __ = ___ P.Y.	

NOTE: It has been my observation that the Path of Life digit added to the age you *will be* this year (or age in any year in question) and reduced to a single digit will equal the Personal Year digit for that year. Use the practice exercise below to work this for yourself. I use this formula as a shortcut when finding Personal Years for the Cycles, too. (1984 for George: age 46 (4+6=1) plus his Path of Life 7 equals 8 P.Y.)

```
                Path of Life Digit

        Age for year you are using  +__

                Total. Reduce.        = __ + __ = ___ P.Y.
```

PERSONAL YEAR INTERPRETATIONS

The following are some of the vibrations of the Personal Years.

1

The time for *new beginnings.* This is the start of a new nine-year cycle. Keep your thoughts on the future and what you want to accomplish over the next nine years. Be independent and original, and activate your plans, your ideals, or your changes. If need be, this is the time to start an entire new life. The future is yours to make now, so plan well and make sure your plan is correct, then take action. This may be the time for renewal of the tried and true. Maybe a change is needed for the betterment of a business or a project that has been successful in the past. This could be an update of plans or a modernization of some part that needs to replace the old and worn. On a more personal note, this may be the time to improve yourself. Cast out any negative vibrations if you have them and start anew. Be independent, positive, ambitious, and have the courage to change. Others are usually involved somewhere and should be taken into consideration when you are doing things that will help them as well. Now is the time to pioneer in that new field, work on that new invention, specialize, or promote that new idea. This year may bring about a move to a new home, a new job or position, or new opportunities to be taken advantage of. Above all else don't be lazy, because this year requires ambition, activity, and push to meet success.

2

Cooperation and *patience* describe this year. This will be a year for partnerships and a willingness on your part to share, since others will have a great deal of influence on your plans and undertakings. Vibrations tend toward harmony and diplomacy. Your patience is required now, so do not try to rush things that are not progressing along as fast as you would like. Things take time, and time is important for development even when it seems to have slowed down. Keep your goals in mind while you work with others, make new friends, be cooperative, receptive and quiet, and things will come to you. Gather all the information you can on subjects that interest you or things that are needed to reach your goal. This year has the vibrations of good friends, love, companionship, and even marriage. If there are negative vibrations this could mean the breakup of partnerships or a divorce. But the 2 is the number of the peacemaker, and if you have patience and understanding you could bring about the peace and cooperation that is needed to bring this situation to better results than even you expected. Any way that you can help others now will also help yourself.

3

This is the year for *self-expression.* Now is the time to show your creativity through words of some kind. Writing, lecturing, acting, or singing may become a part of your life. The 3 is the time for pleasant social activities. You could find yourself traveling or entertaining. Be optimistic and cheerful, and you will find yourself surrounded by your many friends. Be careful not to gossip or talk out of turn, as this could cause problems. Hold on to the goals you set in the 1 Personal Year. You should see some of the results now. This year is a time for working with your inspiration, imagination, and creativity in business or other projects that you may be interested in, giving you financial gain. Show that you have the self-confidence it takes to make a go of any of the opportunities that could open to your talents. You must guard against letting your inner emotions get the upper hand and upsetting you and your plans. Hold the reins on jealousy, resentment, arguments, and harsh words. The scattering of your energies can leave important things undone. This is the year to improve yourself. By keeping a positive attitude you will have a very pleasant year.

4

The opportunities of this year come through *work.* Be practical, orderly, dignified, and patient. Good management is needed in all that you do. This is not the time for laziness or personal pleasure. You will accomplish a great deal, but hard work, common sense, and good organization are a must. Look over your personal and business matters. See what needs to be done in order to place them on a solid foundation. Attend to all matters with detail and honesty, keeping them in order. Repair mistakes from the past; learning from them will strengthen the future. Get an annual health checkup—the 4 is the year to be practical in regards to health because of your heavy work load. Keeping things in order has to do with business, property, insurance or any other legal matters. This is the year to check documents over and make any necessary changes or updates. Good management is a must where money is concerned. This year could have a lot of expenses, but your practicality and thrift will bring you through. This is not the time to trust in luck. This could be a time to buy, sell, build, or trade. Be cautious and read the fine print on all of your transactions. Relatives or in-laws may need a helping hand. Do not allow yourself to become careless or shiftless this year, because if not properly handled, the vibrations of the 4 will fall over into the next year, leaving you little time for the freedom and opportunities of the 5.

5

Change is the vibration of the 5 Personal Year. This year will be made up of new faces, new places, new ideas, or new jobs. This may be the year you will move to a new home. Change will make way for new growth and opportunities. Now is the time to let go of or discard the old or unusable to make way for the new. You may be restless or impatient, wanting more activity, but be careful not to make sudden, hasty decisions that you will be sorry for later. Add variety and versatility to your personal and business interests. You may find you have an interest in the concerns of the public or in world affairs. Keep up with world events, but with an open mind, and use any opportunity that arises here to the best of your ability and for the good of humankind. Be careful not to scatter your forces by having too many irons in the fire. Add a new project to liven up a business. Give advertising a chance. Don't get in a rut. Keep your goal in mind and plan how to advance it now. If others are involved, try to make all changes for their advantage, too. This is a good time to travel for business opportunities or for pleasure. Most of your opportunities are found away from home and regular routine.

6

Responsibility is the key word for this year. Home, family, and community become your obligations now. This is the year of service to others. If you make these efforts interesting for yourself and others, you will find love, friends, warmth, and contentment. If you think only of yourself and personal gains, you will find frustration and regrets later on. When you work for the good of humanity without thinking of personal gains, you will find that rewards will fall into your lap when you least expect it. Spiritual blessings and financial rewards make this a year of success. You may find yourself with the responsibility of caring for a relative, but if this is done to the best of your ability you will find opportunities present themselves to help you with expenses. This may be the year for weddings, children, families, or reunions. Beautify your home or surroundings. If you give love and sympathy you will receive them back, because the 6 needs these. This is the time to buy or build a home. The vibrations of this year lean toward all domestic affairs. Help with civic or community projects. There may be difficulties, misunderstandings, quarrels, and separations in buiness and in your personal life. Children can be a problem now. Love and understanding, honesty, and justice can help most situations. This year can bring about a divorce if there are domestic problems.

7

The vibrations of *knowledge* and *wisdom* travel with you this year. This is a time to rest, take care of your health, and intellectually improve your mind. You will find yourself more alone, but this gives you the quiet time you need to pursue added knowledge for your special interests or talents. The mysteries of life appeal to you this year. You may find yourself interested in science, religion, or metaphysics. Evaluation and self-improvement can be helpful to you. This is a good time to think about your goals and your mission in life. This is not the time for business expansion or change; let things rest where they are for now. Wait for results. This could be the time to travel for health and relaxation or to gain knowledge. Rest, meditation, study, inner strength, quiet pursuits, and better health are vibrating now. Your actions this year could bring misunderstandings and criticism from those around you. They can be unreasonable, but if you try to be reasonable, things should work out. If you work things right, this could be one of the better years in your life, bringing you the recognition you deserve. Learn to enjoy being alone part of the time. Write, think, read, then join groups for educational and philosophical experiences.

8

Achievement vibrates this year. Opportunities for advancement will come your way if you have planned, organized, managed efficiently, and worked hard during the past to reach your goals. Ambition, good judgment, and good business sense are still needed. You are the one who must take the steps in the right direction. Money management is a must, since this could be a year of heavy expenses. Sometimes it takes money to make money. Worry over money can put a mental strain on you, making the year harder to deal with and postponing your achievements. A money management plan should be made at the start of the year to prevent financial disaster. No matter what line of work you are in, this is the time to push some of your ideas and dreams to make improvements and attain success. This is the year for action. You can't gain anything by sitting under a tree and making wishes. This need not be a time to work alone. Advice can come from those in the know if you are not afraid to ask for it. Always be businesslike in your ventures, avoiding emotions and sentimentality. Do not overrate your capability to handle property, investments, or exchanges. Conceit here would cause a downfall. Travel may be necessary now, and you could combine business with pleasure. Don't try to hang on to the material things that have outlived their usefulness. Because they are an asset, you may not want to part with them now, but sometimes it is for the best. Guard your health all year. Avoid dominance in your love life. Success comes through your own efforts. The biggest rewards come when you are doing things for the betterment of all humankind and not thinking of personal gains.

9

Completion is the key vibration this year. This is the time to tie up all the loose ends and make way for the new cycle that starts next year. You are closing a cycle started nine years ago. If you followed through with your plans and dreams by doing the best each year had to offer, you should now be able to see the fruits of your labor. Do the things that have to be done this year to put the finishing touches on your plans and make way for a new cycle to start. All of the good that you have accomplished can be carried over into the next cycle, where you will make plans to add to, expand, remodel, or reinvest. The permanent and durable move forward for continuation until it gets old, useless, inefficient, or outdated. Only things that can be finished in this year should be started now. This is the time to discard the old and worthless things in both your business and personal life. Sometimes this could apply to people that are like a thorn in your side, causing pain and trouble. The 9 usually indicates a loss of some kind. Be willing to let go in the interest of making way for future advancements and happiness. You may have business or friendship losses if you are demanding. Be tolerant, under-standing, and forgiving. Have compassion. This is the time to be doing things for others. Charity and unselfish service to all humankind gives rewards to those who serve without a thought of personal gain. This is the time to restore your health in preparation for all the activity needed in a 1 Personal Year.

Even though a Personal cycle lasts a period of nine years, some people are able to live up to the 11 and 22 Master Numbers when they cycle through their life. For most people these numbers are too hard, so they are reduced to the numbers 2 and 4.

11

This is the year for *inspiration*. This is the year of enlightenment and realiza-tion, which are both needed to find the correct usage of the number 11. If you cannot live up to the 11, you will be living the vibrations of the 2. The 11 is the year for the person who thinks entirely of others. Any new ideals put into use will be for the benefit of all humankind. Let the vibrations of the 11 be used to help those who come to you for guidance. Most who are able to use this Personal Year number are wise, concerned, and have the capabilities to counsel, guide, help, or just listen to those who need an ear. Inner voices and psychic powers, the arts, poetry, or writing could all be inspirational to humankind. This is the year to use your inventive intuition. Materialism would be the downfall here. Personal accumulation is not an 11 vibration. You could be highstrung and show nervous tension this year.

22

Universal is this key vibration. This is the year for the master builder, the one whose project will benefit humanity or the world. Much can be accomplished without limitations when personal concerns are left behind. This is the time to do something good for humankind. Be honest, practical, and use your inspirations for worldwide service. You may find yourself in a leadership position, as director or manager of a large project. This Master Number year is for the big builder, the bridge maker, the one who leads a large corporation, who builds on large scales, or for the average person who has a big project in their life. This Personal Year digit is for the Old Souls who know that the 22 is one of their numbers. They use this vibration to further their causes. When it vibrates, it tells them that now is the time for all the Universal things they know about to be shared with the rest of humankind. 22 is the Universal Number. Keep your views universal, not personal, or you will revert back to the 4 and its work schedule.

The most important alterations and adjustments come in a 1, 5, or 9 Personal Year. Love, marriage, or divorce are felt the strongest in a 2, 5, or 6 Personal Year. The most emotional are the 7 and 9 Personal Years. Hardest times are felt in a 4, 8, or 9 Personal Year, while the largest losses could occur in a 7, 8, or 9 Personal Year. The 3 vibrates creativity. It is the most pleasant year.

PERSONAL MONTH

Like the Personal Year, each month has a different number that it is vibrating to. Knowing what these vibrations are could aid you in using them to enhance your life. The strongest vibrations are felt from the 5th to the 25th of each month. Here again, the past month's vibrations may linger into the first part of the new month long enough to help finish the last month's matters, and the next month's vibrations could be felt on a smaller scale during the last few days of each month.

To find any Personal Month digit, you add the Personal Year digit to the calendar month digit of the month in question.

Write in the month _____ and digit ____ you are using.

(Example: September 9)

(P.Y.)	(from your Personal Year work space)
Plus Month Digit +___	(from above)
Total	= __ + __ = ____ P.M. (PERSONAL MONTH)

The vibrations of the Personal Months are different each year, yet like the Personal Year, the Personal Month has a cycle of nine also. The chart on page 71 shows a full nine-year cycle for both the Personal Years and the Personal Months. Starting with the 1 Personal Year and reading across, January has a 2 Personal

Month, February has a 3 Personal Month, etc. October starts with the same beginning Personal Month digit of the 1 Personal year, then continues the cycle. October, November, and December will always have the same Personal Month digits that January, February, and March started with in that same Personal Year. Also, the first two Personal Month digits are the same as the last two Personal Month digits of the previous year. The month of September will always have the same Personal Month digit as the Personal Year digit because it is a 9 number.

THE 9-YEAR CYCLE FOR PERSONAL MONTHS												
P.Y. DIGIT	**JAN**	**FEB**	**MAR**	**APR**	**MAY**	**JUN**	**JUL**	**AUG**	**SEP**	**OCT**	**NOV**	**DEC**
1	2	3	4	5	6	7	8	9	1	2	3	4
2	3	4	5	6	7	8	9	1	2	3	4	5
3	4	5	6	7	8	9	1	2	3	4	5	6
4	5	6	7	8	9	1	2	3	4	5	6	7
5	6	7	8	9	1	2	3	4	5	6	7	8
6	7	8	9	1	2	3	4	5	6	7	8	9
7	8	9	1	2	3	4	5	6	7	8	9	1
8	9	1	2	3	4	5	6	7	8	9	1	2
9	1	2	3	4	5	6	7	8	9	1	2	3

PERSONAL MONTH INTERPRETATIONS

The following are a few of the Personal Month vibrations.

1

A time to start new things, add to the old, or make changes. Be a leader, not a follower. Use your originality. An active month.

2

Work with others this month. Cooperate, serve others. Partnerships or marriages. Keep peace, arbitrate. This is the month for collecting things.

3

Use your creative talents for self-expression. Make new friends. Seek social activities and entertainment.

4

Work is the key word this month. Build a solid foundation. Do the small, detailed things. Be practical. Place things in order.

5

Many changes. New interests, new people, new places. Travel. Promote new business ideas by advertising. Expand. Don't get in a rut.

6

Shoulder your responsibilities to your home, family, and community. Make your surroundings beautiful. Add music. The month for marriage or divorce.

7

Perfect what you are working on. Use patience. Analyze. Don't talk too much about your projects. Read and study. Gain knowledge. Rest.

8

Use good judgment in all things. Manage your money well, expenses could match income. Add to your business. Many opportunities now.

9

Humanitarian service. Success comes to those who help others without wanting personal gain. A time for selflessness. Tie loose ends.

When the Personal digits are figured out the long way, there is a possibility that they could reduce down to the 11 or the 22. Like the Personal Year, the 11 or 22 Personal Months may be lived with the vibrations of the 2 or 4. It takes a special kind of person to be able to shoulder the vibrations of the 11 or 22. All of humanity and the whole world are the special interests of those with either of these numbers. Their gains come from helping others and working for the good of all.

11

New ideals. Spirituality. Inspiration. New inventions. All actions and thoughts for others. The spotlight may be on you.

22

Building of large projects for the good of humankind. International concerns. Leave personal concerns behind. Big accomplishments.

PERSONAL DAY

Each day of the month has its own Personal Day digit. The Personal Day vibration is indicating what to do on that particular day. Each day has its own vibration, and to do anything against that vibration is unwise. To flow with the numbers brings success.

To find a Personal Day digit, add the Personal Month digit to the calendar day digit in question.
Write in the day you are using _____. Reduce to single digit ____.

P.M. Digit   (from your Personal Month work area)

Day Digit   + __   (from above)

Total   = __ + __ = ____ P.D. (PERSONAL DAY)

Any numbers that were reduced to find the Personal vibrations (also called ESSENCE by some) should be examined as well, since in many cases the primary numbers function as a concealed number of strength. Remember that the higher the number the digit was reduced from, the stronger the vibration.

The vibrations of the Personal Day tell you when the best time is to start something new, help others, work, travel, rest, study, beautify, or wind things up. You must remember to take into consideration the vibrations from the Personal Year (the strongest of these Personal vibrations) and the Personal Month digits. These can help steer you along the correct path on any day. The vibrations of the Universal digits also have background effects and could give just the added touch needed for your day.

A few general do's and don'ts are listed here with their special days.

Best day to start new things	1
The best days for shopping are	1-2-3
Add to checking account	1-2-4-8-22
Good for day off, vacation	3
Advertise; venture; market	5
Buy home; move into it; beautify it	6
Add to savings account	7
Gift-giving; lecturing; finishing touches	9
It is unwise to try to end things that have been started on a	1
Tickets for journeys should not be purchased on	2-4-6
Try not to stay home on this travel day	5
Try not to make long journeys on a	6
Try not to begin things that can't be finished on	6-9
Try not to do many things except review, refine, or rest on a	7
Try not to overspend or be wasteful on an	8

Do all that is necessary on any day.

If you feel the vibrations are not right for the things you want to start or do and you can wait for the correct day, you will have a better chance to succeed by postponing your plans.

PERSONAL DAY INTERPRETATIONS

The following are just a few vibrations for the Personal Days.

1

Start something new. Use your originality. Make appointments and business deals. Find a new job. Trust your own judgment. Use that strong intuition. Today will be very active, and you should be ambitious. This day is for individuality.

2

Work with others today, doing your share. You are the peacemaker. This is the day to add to your collection. Be sympathetic and understanding, not smug and argumentative. Apologize if the need arises. Cooperate.

3

Give a smile to all you meet today. This is your day for self-expression. Be happy. Sing, dance, act, and enjoy this day. Talk but don't gossip. This would be a good day to write. Letters could be answered. Be friendly.

4

This day of work should be planned early and carried out in an orderly manner to get everything done. Put all things around you in order. Be practical in all that you do. Set a firm foundation for the tomorrows.

5

This day of change calls for action on your part; maybe a new job, a new friend, or a new place to see. Variety sets the pace. Advertise, sell, make short trips, or make personal contacts. A good day to do something different.

6

Beautify your surroundings. Shoulder your responsibilities. A good day to look for or buy a new home. Help anyone who needs you, even strangers. Visit the sick. Give advice only when it is asked for; do not intrude.

7

Find some time to be alone today. Rest, meditate. A quiet day in the country could be relaxing. Pause and wait for things to come to you. Try not to be critical of others. Examine your own thoughts and feelings.

8

Accept any opportunities to advance and succeed. Move forward. Material gains could come your way. Show self-confidence. Manage your money well. Do not be overbearing. Do things for others today, it has dividends.

9

This is the day to finish. Tie up all the loose ends. Clear out the old, worn, or useless things in your life. This is a good day for any kind of public performances. Do something for the good of the people.

11

This is not the time to think of personal ambitions. Share your ideals and inspirations with the public. Your knowledge will enlighten others. You are in the limelight. A good day for spiritual activities.

22

Help lighten the burdens of others. Do something that improves things for them. Do things for large groups of people. Follow your hunches. This is not a personal gain day, because you should be working for the good of all humankind.

PERSONAL HOUR

Some people like to figure Personal Hours and use them for making appointments, signing documents, or other personal decisions that relate to their lives.

To find any Personal Hour digit, you add the UNIVERSAL HOUR (U.H.) digit to the PERSONAL DAY digit and reduce if necessary. (Midnight to 1 A.M. is a 1 Universal Hour, 1 A.M. to 2 A.M. is a 2 Universal Hour, etc. The hour from noon to 1 P.M. is a 13 Universal Hour, which reduces to 4; the hour from 11 P.M. to midnight is a 6 Universal Hour [24 reduced to 6].)

Select the Universal Hour you wish to use ____. U.H. digit ____

(Example: 3 P.M. = 15 = 6 U.H.)

P.D.	(from your Personal Day area)
U.H. +__	
Total	= __ + __ = __ P.H. (PERSONAL HOUR)

Use the Personal Day explanation text to find the meanings for the Personal Hours. The number meanings and keywords listed in Appendix A apply here, too.

Personal Pinnacles and Challenges
(Year, Month, Day, Hour)

Each Personal Year, Month, Day, and Hour has its own Pinnacles and Challenges that cycle in much the same way as the Challenges and Attainments used with the birth date, but on a smaller scale. These Pinnacles and Challenges rotate back to their starting cycle every nine years.

Use the Attainment interpretations for the Pinnacle meanings and the Challenge interpretations for all Challenges here. The text in Appendix A for the keywords and the numbers may also be used for added detail.

PERSONAL YEAR PINNACLES
(Attainments or High Points)

There are four Pinnacles for each year, and each Pinnacle lasts three months. The following format is used for any year you may want to know about. We will be using some of these digits over and over again, such as the Birth digit (B.D.), Universal Year digit (U.Y.), Personal Year digit (P.Y.), and Personal Month digit (P.M.). You should be familiar with the format by now, so there won't be any examples. Fill in the blanks below with your dates and single digits.

---

(1)   Digit of year you are using: _____ .

        U.Y.

    Add B.D.   + __

    Reduce   = __ + __ = __ January 1st to March 31st.
                              (Pinnacle duration)

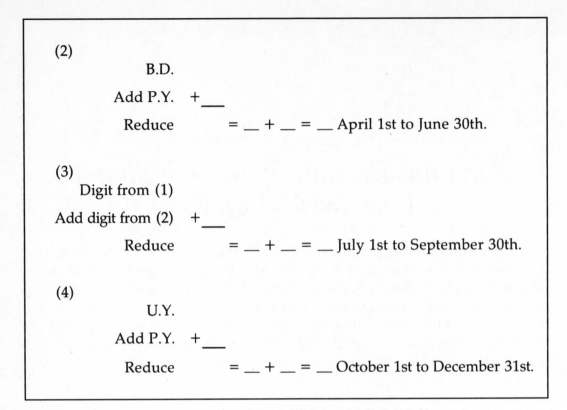

(2)

B.D.

Add P.Y. +__

Reduce = __ + __ = __ April 1st to June 30th.

(3)

Digit from (1)

Add digit from (2) +__

Reduce = __ + __ = __ July 1st to September 30th.

(4)

U.Y.

Add P.Y. +__

Reduce = __ + __ = __ October 1st to December 31st.

PERSONAL YEAR CHALLENGES

As with all the Pinnacles and Attainments, there are challenges that must be learned or moved aside to reach the top. The Personal Year Challenges are worked in the same manner that the Challenges to the Attainments were done. Additional Challenges are used only if the digit found is different from any of the other three Challenge digits. Remember to subtract the smaller digit from the larger digit.

(1)

U.Y.

Subtract B.D. −__

= 1st MINOR CHALLENGE
(vibrates most during first half of year)

(2)

P.Y.

Subtract B.D. $-$___

= 2nd MINOR CHALLENGE
(vibrates most during second half of year)

(3)

Digit from (1)
Subtract digit from (2) $-$___

= MAJOR CHALLENGE
(felt throughout year)

(4)

U.Y.

Subtract P.Y. $-$___

= ADDITIONAL MINOR CHALLENGE
(only if different from other Challenge digits;
felt lightly throughout the year)

PINNACLES FOR PERSONAL MONTH

Digit of Calendar Month you are using _____.

(1)   Duration:

P.Y.

Add Month $+$__

Reduce $=$ __ $+$ __ $=$ __ 1st through 7th of the month.

(2)

P.Y.

Add P.M. $+$___

Reduce $=$ __ $+$ __ $=$ __ 8th through 14th of the month.

(3)

Digit from (1)
Add digit from (2) $+$___

Reduce $=$ __ $+$ __ $=$ __ 15th through 21st of the month.

(4)

Month

Add P.M.   +__

Reduce   = __ + __ = __ 22nd through end of month.

PERSONAL MONTH CHALLENGES

(1)

P.Y.

Subtract Month −__

= FIRST MINOR CHALLENGE
(vibrates during first half of month)

(2)

P.Y.

Subtract P.M. −__

= SECOND MINOR CHALLENGE
(vibrates during second half of month)

(3)

digit from (1)

Subtract digit from (2) −__

= MAJOR CHALLENGE
(felt throughout month)

(4)

P.M.
Subtract Month −__

= ADDITIONAL MINOR CHALLENGE
(If different from other P.M. Challenges;
felt lightly throughout the month)

PINNACLES FOR PERSONAL DAY

Digit of Calendar Day you are using _____.

(1)

	P.M.	Duration:
Add Day +__		
Reduce	= __ + __ = __	From midnight to 6 A.M.

(2)

	P.M.	
Add P.D. +__		
Reduce	= __ + __ = __	From 6 A.M. to noon.

(3)

Digit from (1)

Add digit from (2) +__

Reduce   = __ + __ = __   From noon to 6 P.M.

(4)

	Day	
Add P.D. +__		
Reduce	= __ + __ = __	From 6 P.M. to midnight.

PERSONAL DAY CHALLENGE

(1)

P.M.

Subtract Day −__

= FIRST MINOR CHALLENGE
(vibrates during first half of day)

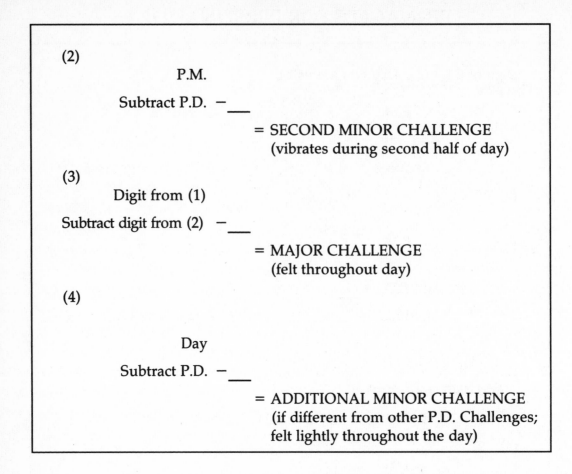

(2)

P.M.

Subtract P.D. − __

= SECOND MINOR CHALLENGE
(vibrates during second half of day)

(3)

Digit from (1)

Subtract digit from (2) − __

= MAJOR CHALLENGE
(felt throughout day)

(4)

Day

Subtract P.D. − __

= ADDITIONAL MINOR CHALLENGE
(if different from other P.D. Challenges;
felt lightly throughout the day)

PINNACLES FOR PERSONAL HOUR

Each hour has four cycles with 15-minute durations. This could indicate the best time to do shopping, gardening, etc. When any of these Pinnacles match a Master Number somewhere in the chart, it gives it a helping hand. I have used the month, day, and hour matching my Path of Life digit for good luck. Test your numbers with important events in your life.

Use the 24-hour clock. Hour you will be using _____ (reduce).

(1)   Duration:

P.D.

Add U.H. + __

Reduce   = __ + __ = __   From top of the hour
to 15 mins. after.

(2)

P.D.

Add P.H. +__

Reduce   = __ + __ = __ Quarter after to half past.

(3)

Digit from (1)

Add digit from (2) +__

Reduce   = __ + __ = __ Half past to quarter to.

(4)

U.H.

Add P.H. +__

Reduce   = __ + __ = __ Quarter to end of the hour.

PERSONAL HOUR CHALLENGES

(1)

U.H.

Subtract P.D. −__

                = FIRST MINOR CHALLENGE
                (vibrates during first half hour)

(2)

P.H.

Subtract P.D. −__

                = SECOND MINOR CHALLENGE
                (vibrates during second half hour)

(3)

Digit from (1)

Subtract digit from (2) −__

                = MAJOR CHALLENGE
                (felt throughout hour)

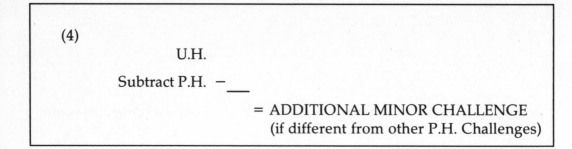

(4)

U.H.

Subtract P.H. $-$__

= ADDITIONAL MINOR CHALLENGE
(if different from other P.H. Challenges)

The secret of success is to adjust the timing of your plans according to which date has the best vibrations for what you want to do. Time and effort are wasted by acting at the wrong times. The Personal Year vibrations and Pinnacles apply to personal matters only. When you have things to do that have or need outside or worldly vibrations, you figure out the Universal Year, Month, or Day digit that matches the date you have in question.

Remember, when working a numerology chart, always take all numbers into consideration, not just the single digits. Any numbers that were reduced to find the Personal vibrations should be examined, because often the primary numbers function as a concealed number of strength. The higher the number that the digit was reduced from, the stronger the vibration.

To make a chart for a Personal Day in one person's life, you need these digits:

The Birth digit and the Universal year
Personal Year, Pinnacles, Challenges   some days these three:
Personal Month, Pinnacles, Challenges   Universal Month
Personal Day, Pinnacles, Challenges   Universal Day
Personal Hour, Pinnacles, Challenges   Universal Hour

Remember that this is just an AVERAGE DAY in an average person's life, so don't let it get out of proportion. Don't leave any digit out when you are interpreting, for you may not get a correct interpretation.

All daily duties must be done regardless of the vibrations. When necessary things are neglected or ignored because of number vibrations, you are not living life as it is supposed to be lived. The vibrations of the numbers are indications for things out of the ordinary, not for necesssary daily chores and duties. For instance, cooks or chefs need to cook, bake, and prepare meals every day, not just days with a 6 vibrating. What needs to be done daily concerning jobs, careers, professions, or any employment must be done in spite of the vibrations of the day. Daily vibrations can possibly add information to or help make decisions in regards to any of these.

These are some of the digits found using the birth date. When you look back at the main worksheet that you have filled in, you will see that Personal Years, Months, Days, and Hours are not there. The worksheet is for permanent digits. We must tell you that the Personal numbers are very important, too. We use them the most, but they change from day to day, so they have no place on the numerology chart.

The worksheet was made for quick reference. When you learn how to do the Personal numbers for the year, month, etc., we know that you will be able to do it without a worksheet and that you will be able to do it at any time. When you use Personal numbers often, it becomes a habit. When they are used day after day, you will soon know what they mean without looking them up.

One special way to keep track of the Personal numbers is to start each new year with a calendar for that year and write in and label your Personal Year digit at the top of each month, then place and label your Personal Month digit for each month next to or under that digit. The Days can be marked for each day by placing your Personal Day digit in the appropriate day square. By doing each month this way, you will have a quick reference for your numbers throughout the year.

For example, say you have a 5 Personal Year. In January of that year (or maybe in December before the new year begins) you would start a new calendar by placing your digit at the top of the sheet for January as "5 Personal Year," and at the top of all the remaining eleven months. The 5 is the Personal Year number for the entire year.

Next you would place your Personal Month digit somewhere at the top of the sheet for January. With a 5 Personal Year digit, the Personal Month digit for January would be a 6, so "6 Personal Month" would be written on January's sheet, "7 Personal Month" on February's, "8 Personal Month" on March's, etc. through the whole calendar.

Now go back to the month of January and write in the Personal Day for each day. The first day of January in a 5 Personal Year and a 6 Personal Month would be a 7 Personal Day, so a "7" would be placed in the bottom of the square for the first day, an "8" in the bottom of the square for January 2nd, a "9" in a day 3's square, and "1" in day 4's square, etc.

Work on through the rest of the calendar. February 1st in a 5 Personal Year and a 7 Personal Month would be an 8 Personal Day, the 2nd would be a 9, etc. By doing this ahead of time and hanging it in a convenient place, you can tell at a glance just what Personal vibrations are in your life for each day.

As mentioned before, the Personal Year digit has the strongest vibration, then the digits of the Month, the Day, and the Hour in that order. When digits match the Personal Year, the vibrations will be stronger and all other digits will give helping hands along the way.

Let's use an example. Let's say the Personal Year is a 5, and you want to know what to expect on January 8th. Looking to the interpretation of the 5 Personal Year, we see that it denotes changes. The Month digit is a 6, so the changes could involve the home, helping others, or other personal responsibilities that you have. The 8th would be a 5 Personal Day, so its vibrations would be stronger because the Personal Year number is 5. This could mean that a bigger change is on the way. The 6 is still quietly vibrating the Personal Month's digit, so that change could be something that is needed around your home, or it could relate to other responsibilities. It could also be a change in a relationship. The 5 and 6 together could mean marriage or a separation. (The 5 would be the change, and 6 is the number for marriages and divorces.)

Once you know what lies ahead, you have the opportunity to act to the best of your ability or to make changes where needed. This is the main purpose of numerology. It directs you. It tells you what could take effect if you do or do not act. For example, say that marriage is in your future. You would want a good, solid 2 or 6 year, number 1 month or day to vibrate good beginnings, or a solid 5 to help ease the transition in your life. The number 6 is the very best vibration for a marriage. When it is put to use, the number 6 makes for better marriages. The number 2 requires cooperation, while the number 6 gives.

There is no one way you would analyze and translate a number. People interpret the same things differently. We each have our own way of doing what needs to be done. Life would be very boring if all the Universe were vibrating to the same interpretation of a number. Therefore, all numbers have several possible interpretations.

The life that you lead must be different from the life someone else leads. We must have our own personality. Being different is what gives us personality. When you are different you live life to the vibrations that you feel.

Each vibration has its purpose. When you understand the basics of numerology you will know what life can hand to you. Understanding and learning is what life is all about.

We all have challenges that we can learn from. When we have learned these lessons well, life could have the smooth path that we all are looking for. We need to recall our challenges once in a while as a reminder, because if we forget a challenge it may come back to teach us again.

PART II

Using The Letters in a Name

The Letters in a Name (Alphabet)

Each letter of the alphabet has an interpretation all its own plus a numeric value that has been assigned to it. Each letter will vibrate to that numeric value and to that letter meaning. (The meaning for each letter is listed in Appendix B, and the numeric values in Appendix A.)

You can use numerology to find the vibrations for people, places or things. In this section of the workbook you will learn how to work with the alphabet. We will start with the full name and its expression. This section teaches the uses and the meanings of the letters in the alphabet.

The numeric values of the English alphabet are as follows:

1	2	3	4	5	6	7	8	9
A	B	C	D	E	F	G	H	I
J	(K)	L	M	N	O	P	Q	R
S	T	U	(V)	W	X	Y	Z	

The letter *K* has a Master Number of 11.
The letter *V* has a Master Number of 22.

We will be using a special form for the name and the three main divisions it holds: the Expression, the Soul Urge, and the Quiet Self. We will be working on each section separately and will put it all together and in the correct order after the Quiet Self is learned.

Expression (Destiny)

The Expression or Destiny digit is found by using the whole name as it is written on the birth certificate. This number describes the way you express yourself to the world. This is you, your whole self—your personality, character, disposition, identity, temperament, your nature.

Always use the full name as it is found on the birth certificate. For an adopted person use the name he or she was born with if it is known. If it is different from the name he/she is using, the first one will always have the strongest vibrations. You should figure both names to see what each is vibrating, because the original name (if known) may be sending out vibrations that are not being understood.

If the person's name has been changed, the original name still gives the strongest vibrations in his or her life. Some people change their names to get better vibrations than the ones they were given at birth. If they had fully understood their birth names and really lived up to the positive vibrations of them, they might not have needed to change them. You choose your name for a purpose before you are born, and you come into this life with something to learn or challenges to overcome. Changing a name may give a few different vibrations, but the first ones are still there needing to be taken care of in this or another lifetime.

When you are figuring a name with *Junior* or *Jr.* in it, use only the first, middle, and last names. Junior is just a designation given with a name and is not used in numerology. (Also note that when figuring the name of a company or business, do not use *Corporation* or *Inc.*)

Using CAPITAL LETTERS, print the full name (exactly as shown on the birth certificate) on the Full Name line below. Place the numeric value for each letter (from the chart above) directly *below* the letters on the Numeric Values line. Add each part of the name separately and reduce to a single digit. Add these three digits together and reduce to get the Expression digit. Use the example for George as a guideline.

FULL NAME: <u>G E O R G E</u> <u>L E S T E R</u> <u>W H I T E S I D E</u>
Numeric Values: 7 5 6 9 7 5   3 5 1 2 5 9   5 8 9 2 5 1 9 4 5

Subtotals: $\frac{39}{3}$ $\frac{25}{7}$ $\frac{48}{3}$
Single digits:

Add. Reduce. <u>3</u> + <u>7</u> + <u>3</u> = <u>13</u> = <u>1</u> + <u>3</u> = <u>4</u>   EXPRESSION (EXPR)

	FIRST	MIDDLE	LAST
FULL NAME:	_____	_____	_____
Numeric Values:			
Subtotals: Single digits:	—	—	—
Add. Reduce.	__ + __ + __ = __ = __ + __ = __		EXPRESSION (EXPR)

EXPRESSION INTERPRETATIONS

1

Leadership, independence, originality, desire to achieve; ambitious, creative, strong, self-reliant, and determined to get on in the world by your own ability. Pioneer, explorer, inventor, director, manager, executive, owner, or head of any business. Those with this number are often writers and lawyers. If on the creative side, many women with this number are found to be dressmakers and designers. They insist upon being left alone to carry out their own ideas. Guard against the negative: egotism, laziness, selfishness, dependence on others.

2

The peacemaker, trouble-shooter, or arbitrator; cooperation. You will usually be in some kind of partnership. Occupations include diplomat, politician, psychologist, student, teacher, secretary, statistician, detail worker, companion, homemaker, artist, psychic, or medium. You could also find interest in religion, banking, science, or cultural things. You work well with others, and perform on behalf of your associates as much as for yourself. You usually marry. Your instinctive rhythm makes you a good musician or dancer. You are fond of detail in your work. Guard against the negative: leaning upon others, apathy, shyness.

3

You are optimistic, outgoing, self-expressing, creative, cheerful, inspirational, popular, social, friendly, artistic, practical. Speaker, writer, singer, entertainer. You use imaginative methods of presentation and are most at home in cheerful and "decorative" occupations. The mental 3 shows natural writing ability; the emotional are actors or singers, the frivolous lean toward society and adornment. Friends are important in your life, and you should cultivate the art of being a true friend. Occupations could also include critic, society organizer or leader, welfare worker, clergy person or missionary, jeweler, milliner, dressmaker, decorator. Guard against the negative: overtalkativeness, boastfulness, gossip, extravagance, jealousy.

4

The worker, the builder, 9 to 5er, the maker of the permanent and the lasting. You are practical and must become proficient in establishing system, order, form, and regulation in your business and personal dealings. Honest, sincere, patient, determined, faithful, and persevering. "System" and "order" should be key words in your life. Care should be taken in your selection of friends. Occupations could include builder, engineer, mason, contractor, electrician, skilled craftsman, technician, economist, statistician, professor, instructor, organizer, executive, accountant, scientist, physician or surgeon, chemist in manufacturing, horticulturist, musician, buyer, salesperson, or administrator. If you deal with hard-to-understand ideas, you must see that they are organized for others to use. Among women with this number are many seamstresses. Also, you will find many household drudges here. You were born to take on responsibilities, and others ask for your support and protection. Build from the ground up. Guard against the negative: destructiveness, carelessness, contrariness, laziness, rigidity, impatience.

5

"Freedom" and "change" are the key words here. You are knowledgeable, outgoing, open-minded, resourceful. Cultivate the resourcefulness and versatility of your makeup. Keep up-to-date and informed about world events. Change to accept the new, and drop the old. Your opportunity comes through people. Your varied interests keep more than one iron in the fire, and you should be careful not to scatter your energies, thereby doing injustice to them all. You are the born traveler. Broaden life by mixing with people of all levels of education, thought, and social activities. Occupations could include traveling salesperson, detective, secret service agent, actor or actress, promoter, inventor, civic leader, senator, lawyer, editor, platform speaker, professional courier, trucker, publicist, advertising person, entertainer, drama critic—occupations that bring you in contact with people. Your free-spirited motto is "The rolling stone gathers no moss." Guard against the negative: irresponsibility, thoughtlessness, over-indulgence (drink, dope, or sex).

6

You are a humanitarian, giving service to others and the world; responsible, understanding, sympathetic, dutiful. Love, charity, truth, justice, harmony, beauty, and companionship describe this 6. Artistic, in tune with nature. Flowers, garden, homes, and parks make a showy display at your touch. You give a helping hand when needed and are generous for the good of others. Occupations include social worker, interior decorator, entertainer, construction worker, writer, farmer, rancher, horticulturist, miner, engineer, dealer in food or home necessities, matron, mother's helper, professional guardian. These are all situations that require responsibility and trust. They are the adjusters and regulators. You will succeed in all occupations connected with homes, institutions, and community or educational activities. You care for the young and old alike and are very community minded. Guard against the negative: pride, insensitivity, jealousy, overbearingness, interference.

7

You are one who seeks knowledge; an educator, philosopher. You must study to test, prove, and gain all the facts about the unknown, unseen, or unproven. Then you will share your findings with all by writing, teaching, or demonstrating the mysteries of life—the hidden, the scientific, or the metaphysical. Because you are a loner and others have a hard time getting to know you, they may think you are different or strange. You live your life according to the truths that you have uncovered, not by the standards set by someone else's system. You will be loved and respected for what you have attained and know. Mix with people who are the thinkers of the world, broaden your opportunities, travel to out-of-the-way places, all in the interest of knowledge. You are a perfectionist. You are at home in any job that doesn't involve physical labor or machinery. Occupations could include educator, lawmaker, scientist, banker, broker, accountant, weaver, watchmaker, inventor, writer of technical, scientific, or philosophical matters, editor, authority on religions, naturalist, astronomer, or metaphysician. Guard against the negative: impatience, secretiveness, miserliness, drink, indifference.

8

Achievement and success in big business, accomplishment in a big way. You need to be in a position of authority and recognition. You would be most successful when involved with the larger material issues of life. Keep your breadth of outlook and admit no limitations. Your pathway will not be an easy one, and your success will come through knowledge, financial effort, and determination. If you learn to work for personal satisfaction and not monetary rewards, you will realize success. When the balance is struck between the spiritual and the material, and you learn to work for the good of all rather than for yourself, you will receive rich rewards. You need to gather great strength of character and mastery over self. You would be wasting your energies searching for wealth. Mental growth comes through investigation and study of religions, the mystical, and philosophy. Businesspersons, writers, literary people, and correspondents should be among your friends. Occupations could include coaching, educating, organizing charities, financier, broker, bondsman, executive, commerical magnate, ship and railroad builder or owner, manufacturer, buyer or seller on a large scale, corporation head, consultant, promoter, newspaper executive, expert on commerce, or anything having to do with navigation or transportation. Guard against the negative: love of power, misspent energy, ambition for material wealth, demand for recognition.

9

You have tolerance, understanding, love, and compassion and will live a life of service to humankind. Your work is at its best when you are free to express your emotions and when inspiration, kindness, and understanding are needed. Your rewards come when you learn that your service is your duty. People from all walks of life will come to you seeking your compassion, understanding, and generosity. Always stay impersonal, for you could lose if you demand power, possessions, and personal love. Don't allow your popularity to go to your head. Having a broad outlook, you are one who hates being confined to small places and small situations (which you make by careless living). Occupations could include teacher, writer, actor, doctor, nurse, lawyer, philanthropist, preacher, reformer, humanitarian, orator, painter, musician, composer, adviser, judge, importer, dramatic actor. Guard against the negative: overemotionalness, self-delusion, harshness, striving for personal gain, insensitivity.

11

You are inspirational, visionary, knowing, original, a leader along spiritual lines. You belong before the public and like to be in the limelight. You are an idealist. You could be a teacher, philosopher, or psychologist—one who digs deep. Occupations include minister, evangelist, religious writer, charity worker, welfare worker, reformer, psychoanalyst, inspired actor, leader, inventor, or explorer. You have an interest in electricity, radio, television, aviation, spiritualism, and metaphysics. You are intuitive and could have psychic abilities. Your high personal ambitions could be your downfall. If living up to the 11 is too hard for you, you may revert to the number 2. Guard against the negative: self above all else, impracticality, irritability, aimlessness, lack of understanding, dishonesty, shiftlessness.

22

This number indicates one who is a master builder. You do all things on a large scale and could launch huge international projects. You have high ideals, are diplomatic, practical and logical; you have your feet firmly on the ground. You are a trailblazer, showing others the way. Occupations could include builder (on a large scale), worldwide shipper, buyer in large quantities for large concerns, leader in international affairs, organizer of public affairs, head of a large institution, diplomat, teacher, ambassador, statesperson, public benefactor, efficiency expert, writer, reformer, or promoter of international projects. You provide service to all. You could be expressing the number 4 if the 22 is too hard to live up to. Guard against the negative: stagnation, rebellion, misdirected energy, inferiority complex.

Soul Urge
(Heart's Desire, Inner Urge, Spiritual Urge)

The Soul Urge describes your innermost person—your hopes, dreams, longings, soul motivations, and desires. This Soul Urge may be known to you, but you may not be expressing it outwardly or living it. You could be depressing your inner feelings or urges—what you would like to be or do, your secret goals and ambitions.

For this exercise we will print out the name again. This time we will be adding the value of the VOWELS only. The vowels and the Soul Urge are figured ABOVE the name, so you are working from the bottom up, so to speak. Write the numeric value of each vowel only directly above the vowel on the Vowel Values line (use the letter *Y* as a vowel if you feel it is used as a vowel in the sounding of the name). Add the first name vowel values and reduce to a single digit. Do the same for the middle name and the last name. Place the subtotals for each part above the subtotal line. Reduce each subtotal to a single digit and place it on the SU digits line. Add these three digits and reduce to get the Soul Urge digit, or SU.

Using our sample again, we find that the Soul Urge for George is 9.

SU digits:	<u>7</u>	+	<u>1</u>	+	<u>1</u> = 9 SU
Subtotals:	16		10		28
Vowel Values:	<u>5 6</u> <u>5</u>	<u>5</u> <u>5</u>		<u>9</u> <u>5</u> <u>9</u> <u>5</u>	
FULL NAME:	G E O R G E	L E S T E R		W H I T E S I D E	

Figure the Soul Urge for the name you are using.

SU digits:	__	+	__	+	__ = __ SU
Subtotals:	__		__		__
Vowel Values:	_____	_____		_____	
FULL NAME:					

95

SOUL URGE INTERPRETATIONS

1

You have an inner urge to be creative and original. You are capable of creating great accomplishments on a large scale. Being independent, you want to choose your own pursuits, work alone, or be your own boss. You have a pioneering spirit and want to explore. You are honest and loyal and crave intellectual challenges. You create opportunities for others to praise your abilities. You want to be heard. You may want to work on inventions or scientific projects.

2

You desire companionship, partnership, love, marriage, and understanding. To attract the friendships that you want, you try to be kind and thoughtful toward others. You prefer to follow rather than lead, so you work for and with others. You guard against criticism from others, fearing the unhappiness it brings. Often those with the number 2 have psychic abilities they would like to develop. Some would like to seek careers in art or music. Some would like to be the shoulder that others cry on.

3

You desire self-expression through speaking, acting, or writing. You strive to be friendly, outgoing, independent, ambitious, fearless, artistic, intuitive, inspirational, humorous, and expressive. You want beauty, joy, and happiness all around. Some of you love children and wish to work anywhere they are involved. Some have a desire to work with pets. Some wish to be artistic painters.

4

You value order and regularity in work and at home. You are excellent with details but want work cut out for you. You need recognition from others and have a strong desire to always be correct. You want to create constructive projects that help humanity and bring you success. You want your life partner to be very practical-minded in order to match your goals of a permanent foundation for home and family. You want to be considered as conscientious, methodical, thorough, dependable, practical, analytical, and determined. You have a desire to use your natural mechanical ability and work with your hands. You like to be able to take your time in order to do things well.

5

You desire change, adventure, travel, and new interests involving the exciting and unexpected. You may feel restless and impatient because of your desire for personal freedom and your determination not to let others regulate your ideals or your life. You yearn to get away from the everyday routine because it is very boring to you. You want the changes that come with having many irons in the fire, even though it would scatter your energy, time, and money and result in things being left undone. You have an intellectual bent and want to learn about all the phases of life. You can adapt to any condition, class of people, or country. With a 5 Soul Urge you may want to do unexpected things at a moment's notice, such as taking a trip, moving to a new home, changing jobs, etc.

6

You seek responsibility, love, home, and family, with the self as the center of attention. You want your surroundings to have beauty, comfort, music, harmony, and peace. You would like to be able to help all of humankind when your help is needed. You want to be considered as sympathetic, an idealist, frank, just, and the peacemaker. You would like your viewpoints, your way of doing things, or your beliefs to be considered as correct. You do more for others in hopes that by doing so it will help you become popular. You want to display your artistic talents. You desire to work with others, never alone. You help others to get the appreciation and thanks they crave. You dream of having a good speaking or singing voice. You would like to be a good counselor and friend.

7

You desire the knowledge and wisdom of all things, including the mysteries of life that lure you. You would like to delve deep to find the truth, and you desire solitude so that you can have the environment needed for your quest of knowledge. You want everything and everybody to measure up to the way you think life should be. You desire perfection. You desire the best life has to offer. You would like to be understood for the way you think. You would like to be knowledgeable on all levels. Because the mysteries of the spiritual or metaphysical worlds fascinate you, you would like that deep intuitive feeling you have about things to help you delve into these mysteries of life. You prefer not to do manual labor. You desire to share with others while looking for true happiness. You desire rest and relaxation when you want it.

8

You want to do all things in a big way. You would like to be manager, supervisor, director, executive, leader, or owner of your own business. You want to lead, not follow. With this number you would like to be important. Some have the desire to work with money in banks, loan offices, financial firms, or with stocks and bonds. A desire to become an accountant fits this number. Working in important places such as government, county, or city offices is the desire of some 8's. Some long to become architects and draft blueprints for tall buildings, shopping centers, or other large building projects. Some would like to be able to manage their lives just as they see fit. Most would like to be known for their sound judgment and excellent planning ability.

9

Being the number of the humanitarian, you want to help others. You want to serve the whole world. You would like to be known as generous, self-sacrificing, kind, and always ready to teach or give without a second thought. You want all to benefit from your knowledge and experiences. You want to be compassionate and selfless. You would like to work with or be involved in some aspect of music or the arts, even if it is just to enjoy. You want to be independent. Some would like to be healers. Some would like to be counselors, possibly working with those less fortunate. There is a desire vibrating with this number to do what can be done for others when it is needed, leaving personal matters in the background. Nines need to be needed. They have a desire for love, home, and happiness. Many would like to be caretakers of the young or elderly. Some desire to manage property and estates.

11

You desire to be an inspiration to all. You want to inspire and bring light to the masses through art or science. Some with this number have the desire to explore the mystical side of life. Others would like to promote their psychic abilities in some way. Some desire a spiritual way of life. Some want to be leaders and to be in the limelight. If this number does not fit your feelings, you could be the number 2.

22

You want to be the master builder for the good and security of all. Some 22's dream of being engineers, architects, bridge builders, highrise builders, dam builders, or creators of other expansive undertakings. Some desire to be the masters of every situation. Others would like to find a niche in large undertakings, serving large groups of people or helping the world through diplomatic services or leadership. If the 22 is not your vibration, you may be the number 4.

Quiet Self
(Quiescent, Latent Self, Inner Self)

The Quiet Self is a power or quality that is hidden within and may not be recognized by you. The Quiet Self is the motivating force within that helps you to achieve, create, or reach a goal in your life. This is the inner being at rest or in a dormant state. Although concealed inside, it can rise and reveal itself at any time. It is always present but not visible or active. It is the daydreamer, schemer, planner, the doer or builder inside you that is not always showing, even to your family or friends.

Figure the Quiet Self in the same manner as the Soul Urge, but use the lines *below* the full name. Using the full name again, we will be adding the value of the CONSONANTS only. Write the numeric value of each one directly below the full name (use the letter *Y* here if it is not used as a vowel). Add the first name values and reduce to a single digit. Do the same for the middle and the last name. Add these three digits together and reduce to a single digit. This digit is the Quiet Self, or Q.S.

Again we are using our sample for George.

FULL NAME:	G E O R G E	L E S T E R	W H I T E S I D E
Consonant Values:	7 9 7	3 1 2 9	5 8 2 1 4
Subtotals:	23	15	20
QS digits:	5 +	6 +	2 = 13 = 4
			QUIET SELF (QS)

Now fill in the blanks below with the name that you are using and find the digit for the Quiet Self.

FULL NAME:	_____	_____	_____
Consonant Values:			
Subtotals:	__	__	__ = =
QS digits:	+	+	QUIET SELF (QS)

QUIET SELF INTERPRETATIONS

Listed below are some inner dreams or potentials for each Quiet Self number.

1

Has a secret ambition for leadership or achievement; wants to do something original, to follow the inner voice.

2

Dreams of peace and harmony. Companionship, home, and family are important, with self quietly serving in the background.

3

Wishes for self-expression in a creative way. Wants to be attractive, popular, and appreciated.

4

Wants to work or build endlessly for reward, love, and appreciation.

5

Dreams of being free to travel unhampered, to live for adventure and experience.

6

Dreams of a beautiful home and the devoted love of a family, with the self as the center.

7

Dreams of a place of quietude, surrounded by books for knowledge and contemplation. Wishes to be a teacher, priest or mystic whose mind is full of ancient wisdom.

8

Dreams of being the BIG businessperson, doing everything on a grand scale.

9

Wants to understand the suffering of others, wishes to be of service to the needy. Is sought out for solace. Artistic.

11

Dreams of enlightening the world by inspiring others with knowledge from higher planes.

22

Dreams on the largest of all scales: big buildings, big factories, anything constructive and for the benefit or enjoyment of all.

VERIFICATION AND APPLICATION: SU, QS, AND EXPR

Let's take a moment to double check our figures. If you add the Soul Urge digit to the Quiet Self digit and reduce to a single number, you should come up with the same digit as the Expression. If these digits do not match, then you know that there is an error in your figuring somewhere. Use the following example and the space below to verify your figures.

George has a 9 Soul Urge digit and a 4 Quiet Self digit.

Example: $9 + 4 = 13 = 1 + 3 = 4$, the Expression digit for George.

__ + __ = __ = __ + __ = __ your Expression digit.

We can now put together a whole chart for the Expression, Soul Urge, and Quiet Self that looks like the form on page 102. Starting at the center, write in the full name first. It is easier to look at if you use all capital letters. Next write the numeric value of each letter in the spaces directly below the letters. Now you have all of the values in one place and it is easier to copy the correct values to the Expression, Soul Urge, and Quiet Self rows. Refer to George's example when needed.

After you have completed the chart, place the digits for the Expression, Soul Urge, and the Quiet Self in the Name Vibs. (Vibrations) column on the worksheet in the front of this book. Place each digit under its appropriate SU, EXPR, and QS abbreviation.

SU digits:		$\frac{7}{16}$	+	$\frac{1}{10}$	+	$\frac{1}{28}$ = 9 SU
SU subtotals:						

VOWELS: 5 6 5 5 5 9 5 9 5

FULL NAME: <u>G E O R G E</u> <u>L E S T E R</u> <u>W H I T E S I D E</u>
NUMERIC VALUES: 7 5 6 9 7 5 3 5 1 2 5 9 5 8 9 2 5 1 9 4 5

EXPR subtotals: $\frac{39}{3}$ + $\frac{25}{7}$ + $\frac{48}{3}$ = 13 = 4 EXPR
EXPR digits:

CONSONANTS: 7   9 7   3   1 2   9   5 8   2   1   4
QS subtotals: $\frac{23}{5}$ + $\frac{15}{6}$ + $\frac{20}{2}$ = 13 = 4 QS
QS digits:

SU digits: ___ + ___ + ___ = SU
SU subtotals:
VOWELS:

FULL NAME: _____ _____ _____
NUMERIC VALUES:

EXPR subtotals: ___ + ___ + ___ = = EXPR
EXPR digits:

CONSONANTS:
QS subtotals: ___ + ___ + ___ = = QS
QS digits:

This same format can be used to figure the vibrations of a country, state, city, town, or any place that has a name you are interested in. Their meanings would be interpreted from the vibrations of the keywords in Appendix A. This would tell you if their numbers are the vibrations you are looking for or if they match or help any of your main numbers. General interpretations of the numbers may be used here also.

Name Challenges

Like the birth date, the name expresses Challenges. And like the Challenges of the birth date, Name Challenges teach lessons that you came into this world to learn. When you were born you chose the name you were born with in order to overcome certain obstacles or learn something that is lacking in the vast knowledge you store in your subconsciousness. Your name vibrates what you are and what you came to learn.

Like all Challenges, the smaller digit is subtracted from the larger digit no matter which line in the work area it has been placed upon. The Name Challenge meanings can be found in the interpretations at the end of the Life's Challenges section.

SOUL URGE CHALLENGE

Using the full name again, the Soul Urge Challenge is found by subtracting the digit of the first vowel in the first name from the digit of the last vowel in the last name (the smaller number from the larger). This digit is the Soul Urge Challenge.

Using the name of George Lester Whiteside as our example, we find:

First Vowel in First Name = E   5 (numeric value of E)

Last Vowel in Last Name = E   −5 (numeric value of E)

=   0 SOUL URGE CHALLENGE

Fill in the blanks below with the vowels from the name you are working with, and write in their numeric values. Subtract to find the Soul Urge Challenge.

First Vowel in First Name = ___   ___ (numeric value)

Last Vowel in Last Name = ___   −___ (numeric value)

___ SOUL URGE CHALLENGE

QUIET SELF CHALLENGE

The Quiet Self Challenge is found by subtracting the value of the first consonant in your name from the value of the last consonant in your name. This digit is the Quiet Self Challenge.

Using George's name again we find:

First Consonant in Name = G   7 (numeric value of G)
Last Consonant in Name = D   − 4 (numeric value of D)
                                 ___
                               = 3 QUIET SELF CHALLENGE

Fill in the blanks below using the first and last consonants from the name you are using. Write in their numeric values and do the figuring for the Quiet Self Challenge.

First Consonant in Name = ___   ___ (numeric value)

Last Consonant in Name = ___ − ___ (numeric value)

=   QUIET SELF CHALLENGE

EXPRESSION CHALLENGE

The Expression Challenge is found by subtracting The Soul Urge Challenge digit from the Quiet Self Challenge digit.

Using the digits that were found by using George's name, we have:

Soul Urge Challenge   0
Subtract Quiet Self Challenge   −3
                              ___
                            = 3 EXPRESSION CHALLENGE

Fill in the blanks below with the digits from the name you are using, and figure the Expression Challenge.

Soul Urge Challenge

Subtract Quiet Self Challenge − ___

= ___ EXPRESSION CHALLENGE

Place your digits in the Name Challenge column on the worksheet on page 4. Put each digit under its appropriate abbreviation.

Inclusion (Intensification)

The Inclusion chart is an important chart in numerology. It can reveal how you direct your life, uphold your responsibilities, and use your abilities because it explains why or how you react to each number vibration. The Inclusion is a personality chart, so to speak; it tells you about your general characteristics, inclinations, and minor traits, what your abilities and talents are, what you work best at, and what will be expected of you. It also tells you where your strengths and weaknesses are. The Inclusion chart uses all the letters in your entire name.

HOW TO MAKE AN INCLUSION CHART

To complete an Inclusion chart you need to know the distribution of the number values in your name. In other words, you must count how many times each number shows up in your name. Using George's name as an example (21 letters in all), we come up with the following breakdown:

FULL NAME:	G E O R G E	L E S T E R	W H I T E S I D E
NUMERIC VALUES:	7 5 6 9 7 5	3 5 1 2 5 9	5 8 9 2 5 1 9 4 5

Letters having a numeric value of 1: **2**
Letters having a numeric value of 2: **2**
Letters having a numeric value of 3: **1**
Letters having a numeric value of 4: **1**
Letters having a numeric value of 5: **7**
Letters having a numeric value of 6: **1**
Letters having a numeric value of 7: **2**
Letters having a numeric value of 8: **1**
Letters having a numeric value of 9: **4**

Total equals the number of letters in the full name: **21**

Fill in the blanks below with the full name that you are working with and place the numeric values below each letter. Then write the total for each number group in the appropriate spaces (place a 0 on the line of any missing number).

FULL NAME: _____ _____ _____

NUMERIC VALUES:

Letters having a numeric value of 1: __

Letters having a numeric value of 2: __

Letters having a numeric value of 3: __

Letters having a numeric value of 4: __

Letters having a numeric value of 5: __

Letters having a numeric value of 6: __

Letters having a numeric value of 7: __

Letters having a numeric value of 8: __

Letters having a numeric value of 9: __

Total equals the number of letters in the full name ____

For eye appeal and easy access, the next form is set up like a tic-tac-toe chart. This is the form used for the Inclusion chart interpretation. The correct number placements are shown below.

Number Placement

1's	2's	3's
4's	5's	6's
7's	8's	9's

George's Chart

2	2	1
1	7	1
2	1	4

Fill in the tic-tac-toe chart for your name. If a number is missing, place a 0 in that square.

Number Placement				Your Chart		
1's	2's	3's				
4's	5's	6's				
7's	8's	9's				

Now you can see at a glance which numbers have an average amount, an over-abundance, or a shortage. Using your Inclusion chart and Inclusion interpretations that follow, check all nine numbers for their traits. Average amounts will be 2 or 3 in most names. The number 5, being the most-used number, usually has a large amount of letters. Some numerologists subtract 2 from a number 5 total. In a large name, 4 or 5 may be an average number and 2 would indicate a shortage or few.

Always read the Inclusion interpretations for the indications they show even though lacking numbers could be vibrating from elsewhere in your numerology chart, waiting to give their vibration where needed if and when called upon.

By coincidence, our example of George uses all nine numbers. His high or overabundant number would still be 5, even after subtracting 2 from the 7 amount. The number 9 is high also. Numbers 1, 2, and 7 border on the average to few. (In this case read both explanations to see if one suits the person better than the other.) The 3, 4, 6, and 8 would be classified as few or a shortage.

INCLUSION INTERPRETATIONS

1

AVERAGE AMOUNTS: Self-assurance, aggressiveness, pride, originality, creativity, determination, initiative and will power. Qualities of leadership and the individuality necessary to get along in this life.

TOO MANY 1's: Ability to accomplish things. Shows domination, great deal of courage; fixed ideas, independence, strong opinions, and vigorous energy. Stands up for own rights with strong will power and is occasionally assertive or could be effective with silence. Witty and humorous. Original thinker. Leadership with an inclination to govern and a persistence to control.

FEW OR NONE: Self is not of importance, unable to stand alone, does not have enough confidence or self-drive, short in ambition and initiative. Easy to associate with, charming, more interested in others.

2

AVERAGE AMOUNTS: Instinctively wants to associate with others; friendly, good mannered, cooperative.

TOO MANY 2's: Peacemaker, romantic, friend; has a sense of timing and rhythm. Sensitive, emotional, desires companionship; may be timid and reserved, could become a doormat. Many 2's in a man's name could designate a genteel nature. The ability to do things well, to gather information with patience and skill is characteristic of this nature. Interest in history and things of the past.

FEW OR NONE: Lack of consideration, crabby, edgy, touchy, unrefined, oversensitive, uncooperative, inflexible.

3

AVERAGE AMOUNTS: Creativity, vivid imagination, enthusiasm, friendliness. Outgoing, self-important. Ability to express in written or spoken words, likes to do big things. A happy, sociable number.

TOO MANY 3's: Impatience, extravagance, carefreeness, boastfulness, talkativeness, or overemotionalness could lead to wasted endeavors. Talented in many ways. Inspiration, imagination, mastery of word. Does not like hard, physical work, but if inspired will work patiently and perseveringly to get results. Admiration, romance, and popularity are very important.

FEW OR NONE: Inferiority complex, lacks the ability to express, lacks showmanship. Withdrawn.

4

AVERAGE AMOUNTS: Concentration and proper application give the ability to work hard and maintain order and objectivity.

TOO MANY 4's: Good concentration ability. Smothers self with too many detailed or mundane tasks, yet has the ability to survey, assess and to recognize the merit of necessary and objective plans and put ideas into form. Understands detail, has a willingness to work. In-laws could be a pleasure or the problem. Fours are often stubborn and narrow-minded.

FEW OR NONE: Dislikes work, order, system, and routine. Displays impatience. Could be lazy. Help and assistance will come through others.

5

AVERAGE AMOUNTS: Accepts change, desires adventure and variety, has an awareness of the appropriate use of personal freedom.

TOO MANY 5's: Restless nature, lack of application, interest in too many things, moving from one job or line of work or interest to another without completing either. Could misuse personal freedom and possibly cause others pain and suffering. Many 5's could become overindulgent in matters of sex. Usually restless, rushed, impetuous. Loves excitement and has a worldly interest in all things.

FEW OR NONE: Unable to accept change, dislikes crowds, has limited life experiences; lacks inquisitiveness, understanding, and adaptability. Is jealous, wants to be left alone.

6

AVERAGE AMOUNTS: Humanitarian, responsible; loves home, beautiful surroundings, the luxuries and comforts of life. Could be idealist, teacher, healer, medical aide or involved in the care or welfare of others. Is usually well groomed. Adjusts well to most situations. Has a sharp awareness of the ethical and unethical.

TOO MANY 6's: Willingly accepts responsibility, gives generously, and is a fine humanitarian. Has strong opinions and is stubborn, with inflexible standards and principles. May be overconcerned about family responsibilities. May become bewildered or heartbroken if their standards are not met or are disregarded. Strongly traditional, sometimes has fanatical nature.

FEW OR NONE: Aversion to responsibility and duty, has a hard time accepting things at their face value. Could display personal and selfish interests. May be domineering with family. This number is often found elsewhere in the chart.

7

AVERAGE AMOUNTS: Keen mind, analyzing and questioning, understanding and compassionate. The number of technique, observation, precision, discrimination, and the ability to explore the unknown.

TOO MANY 7's (very rare): The number of the specialist who has great intellectual capacity. These are the investigators, the inventors, the seekers of hidden truths. They are difficult to get to know and understand. Are secretive and selective. Usually have a few well chosen, knowledgeable friends.

FEW OR NONE: This would be a person with a more outgoing personality than a seven holds. This person would not be searching each and every nook and cranny for hidden meanings. They find inner peace, search for personal faith, happiness, and are openminded.

8

AVERAGE AMOUNTS: Has an appreciation for material things. Self-efficient and enterprising, with an ability to administer, manage, and supervise others—generally a leader or in authority. Seems to dominate, leans toward independent activity and reasoning, observes both sides. Good in emergencies. Needs good judgments where business and money are concerned.

TOO MANY 8's: Can organize and coordinate the work of others. These are the supervisors, the floor-walkers, the overseers, often counselors. Some may be over-obsessed with the want of wealth or material things. Most are good judges of character and have good standing in the community. This life could be full of personal tests that involve proper management of money or desire of power.

FEW OR NONE: No interest in jobs where finances are concerned. May lack the ability to manage money. Does not have the desire or need for material things. Depends on others in most situations.

9

AVERAGE AMOUNTS: Kindness, toleration, humanitarianism. Wants and gives love and charity; is generous and sympathetic. Understands all walks and all levels of life.

TOO MANY 9's: Overemotional, impressionable, imaginative, generous—often to extremes; lack of direction and balance. Could be someone who gives too much or does too much for someone who should be helping themselves. May be very opinionated. Always determined to do their own thing.

FEW OR NONE: Not as caring or compassionate as most nines. Must be helped at times in their life. Has the kindness and capabilities yet lacks the sense to know when help should be given.

Ruling Passion
(Hidden Passion, Secret Desire)

The Ruling Passion is the strong inner drive you feel that compels you to act. It could indicate a special hidden desire to do something you enjoy most. Some persons find that this powerful force within should be kept in check so that its strong vibration does not become too dominant or overimportant in their lives.

The Ruling Passion digit is found by using the Inclusion chart to see which number or numbers appear the most. Some people may have more than one number that appears with greater frequency. Usually the number 5 is the most prominent in all charts because the letters *E* and *N* are the most commonly used in the English alphabet; therefore, subtract 2 from the number in the 5's square before deciding which number (or numbers) is the Ruling Passion.

Looking at George's chart we find that he has seven 5's. Even after we have subtracted 2 from that 7, it leaves the number 5 as having the highest total, so George's Ruling Passion digit is 5.

Look over your Inclusion chart again. Which square(s) has the highest total? If there is more than one number with the same high total, there is more than one Ruling Passion digit. (Some people may have three or four digits with the same high total but this does not happen often.)

Now fill in the blank or blanks below with the number or numbers that have the same highest digit.

Ruling Passion digit(s): _____ _____ _____ _____

To find quick interpretations for the Ruling Passion, place the words *compelling drive for* in front of the numeric keywords in Appendix A.

RULING PASSION INTERPRETATIONS

A Ruling Passion could be one or more of the following vibrant, sometimes compelling, drives within.

1   A powerful, urging drive for yourself.
2   A compulsive drive for affiliation, association, or fellowship.
3   A drive for your original, creative expression.
4   A workaholic-like drive for work.
5   A drive for freedom of choice and personal independence.
6   A drive for responsibility of home, marriage, or position.
7   A drive for knowledge, wisdom, understanding.
8   A drive for money, power, material things.
9   A drive for universal knowledge, all-encompassing love. A drive to do one's own thing.

CHALLENGES TO THE RULING PASSION

These Challenges teach what you must learn to do in this life to make up for a weakness or deficiency. They are indicated by the 0's or missing numbers in the Inclusion chart. When you see numbers missing it denotes something missing in life or lessons to be learned. If the missing number is found in other places of the numerology chart, that Challenge will be lightened. Any square in the Inclusion chart with a 0 in it denotes a Challenge. Some names do not have any, while others have more than one.

Some numerologists say a 0 here, or a missing number elsewhere, denotes lessons learned in a previous lifetime. We say it is impossible for us to work back from this lifetime to see what was taught. We say no one can know, in all good faith, just what vibrations are from the past. Numerology is pointing to what should be learned in this lifetime.

In our chart for our example of George we find no 0's. Here George would have no special challenge.

Look at your Inclusion chart and write down which number or numbers show a 0.

Your Ruling Passion Challenge digit(s): _____ _____ _____ _____

RULING PASSION CHALLENGE INTERPRETATIONS

A number 9 can be a Challenge here, so we will use a special Challenge interpretation text for the Ruling Passion Challenges. If you have more than one Challenge digit, be sure to read each one.

1

Zero in the 1 square denotes a need to gain self-confidence. You need to learn to do things on your own. Make decisions, become more ambitious and aggressive. Use your initiative and originality.

2

Zero in the 2 square denotes a need to learn to cooperate with others. Come out of your shell, meet people. Get over your shyness. You must learn to work with others.

3

Zero in the 3 square denotes a need to learn to express yourself. You need to build your self-confidence. Curb your temper. You need to learn to get out into the public.

4

Zero in the 4 square denotes a need to learn good work habits. You must learn to manage in an orderly manner. You must learn how to apply yourself, even to the small details.

5

Zero in the 5 square denotes a need to accept change. You need to curb your desire for freedom without responsibilities. You need to overcome impatience.

6

Zero in the 6 square denotes a need to accept responsibilities. You must learn the responsibilities of home, family, and service to others. Many adjustments are needed for a good marriage or partnership.

7

Zero in the 7 square denotes a need to learn, gain knowledge. You jump to conclusions. Develop patience and understanding. Have faith, not fear. Balance the material and spiritual.

8

Zero in the 8 square denotes a need to manage money, time, material, or business affairs wisely. You must learn that material things belong to everyone.

9

Zero in the 9 square denotes a need to learn compassion. You will have many ups and downs until you learn to help others and be sympathetic, kind, and generous. The self comes second here.

Subconscious Self

The Subconscious Self is who you are as a human being—how you respond to situations and relationships. It indicates the subconscious reaction you have in an emergency or crisis situation. Or it could be your immediate reaction or thought when faced with a challenge or new venture.

The Subconscious Self is emotional rather than mental. It does not indicate ability, nor does it represent conscious urges or impulses. It is like an aura around you and is usually more apparent to your friends than to yourself.

The Subconscious Self digit is found by subtracting the number of 0's (how many—not which numbers have 0's) in the Inclusion chart from the number 9. Using the Inclusion Chart again, count the number of 0's or missing numbers and subtract that number from 9. This is the Subconscious Self number.

Using George's chart we find no 0's. His number will be 9.

Fill in the blanks below for the name you are using.

Use the BASE number of 9	9
Subtract how many are 0's	−__ (Very few have none.)
SUBCONSCIOUS SELF NUMBER	__

SUBCONSCIOUS SELF INTERPRETATIONS

1, 2, 3

These numbers are never found in an Inclusion chart. If a 3 were found, it would mean six lessons, which is a hard life to live. There would be a tendency to fight for expression against constant opposition, which would almost always result in destructive reactions.

4

This vibrates someone who uses mental energy to organize, manage, and help. The 4 takes whatever time is necessary to put it all together. Once satisfied that you have accomplished what was necessary, then you will act.

5

This person is unpredictable, anxious, and unsure. A lot of turmoil with little change. Inconsistent, thoughtless, and forever demanding variation.

6

This person's first responsibility would be to home and family. Once these are stabilized, care and understanding for others who need it can be established.

7

A well of secrecy. Detached, preoccupied, sensitive, unconcerned. Refers things to the inner self and hopes for the best. Could take to drink. Inwardly responds to love but outwardly throws cold water on it.

8

Refers things to concrete facts or reason. Rather cold and matter of fact but very dependable and solid; could be relied upon in almost any situation.

9

This person would be rather bored with life because everything has been done at least once. Impersonal, shows little concern, interested in a little of everything but excited by nothing special. Has a critical viewpoint.

PART III

Using the Birth Date
and/or the Name

Cornerstone

The Cornerstone is the being or entity around which you are built or founded—your basic element, or essentials that you came into life with. It has an impact on your everyday disposition and relates to how you interpret your life experiences. It either helps or restrains the Expression.

The first letter in the first name is the Cornerstone. Use both the numeric meanings in Appendix A and the alphabet meanings in Appendix B for the explanation.

George's first letter is G, so his Cornerstone is 7.
Fill in the blanks for the name you are using.

First letter in first name is ____. Numeric value ____ = **Cornerstone.**

The Key (Number)

This number is a guidepost showing how the vibrations of your first name influence your way of life. The Key is found by reducing all the numeric values of the first name letters only. Each letter has a transit vibration (explained in the Excursion section) that can show if and when periods of great accomplishment will occur or if the person must either keep trying to adjust or wait patiently for the door to be opened. The numeric values in Appendix A are used for the Key meanings.

Look back to the worksheet where we figured the Expression.
Use the single-digit total of the first name only (George = 3).

First name total (single digit only) ____ = **The Key.**

Eccentricity

The Eccentricity shows how a person responds to everyday relationships, or how life is lived when a certain problem (unsolvable or unpleasant) brings disagreeable circumstances.

The Eccentricity is found by adding the day of birth digit to the Key digit (the total of all the numbers in the first name only). The meanings are in the Eccentricity text that follows the work area.

Our sample for George:

$$\begin{array}{rl} \text{Day of Birth} & 20 \\ \text{Key digit} & +\ 3 \\ \hline \text{Total. Reduce to single digit.} & 23 \end{array} \quad = 2 + 3 = 5 \text{ Eccentricity.}$$

Fill in the blanks below with your numbers.

Day of Birth	____
Key digit	+ ___
Total. Reduce to single digit	_____ = __ + __ = __ **Eccentricity.**

ECCENTRICITY INTERPRETATIONS

These numbers show some of the ways that people respond to unexpected problems.

1   Relates everything to self. Tries to master everything without help. Prefers to stand alone.

2   Would look to others for a helping hand. Togetherness, or "two heads are better than one," describes the 2.

3   Creative. Comes up with original ideas to solve situations.

4   Tries to work everything out to their satisfaction.

5   Would like to change things around and still have personal freedom. Willing to try something new and take a chance.

6   Accepts responsibility, but takes care of family and home first. Tries to meet all obligations.

7   Mentally analyzes. Seeks divine guidance. Uses inside reflection. Waits for development.

8   Plans before acting. Organizes and keeps aim in mind at all times while acting. Drives toward material gain or advancement.

9   Called the Brotherhood of Man, the 9's viewpoint has the good will of all humanity in mind before making any decisions.

Key Letter (Second Key)

The Key Letter represents a specific personal quality or goal that you aim for. It is taken from the numeric value of the first letter in the last name (surname). For George that is *W*, which equals 5.

> First letter in last name ____. Numeric value _____ = **Key Letter**

Use the numeric interpretations in Appendix A for the Key Letter's meaning.

Balance Number

This number is the one that you use in emergencies to stabilize yourself, or that you apply to hold your balance. This number is found by adding the numeric values of all three initials of the full name and reducing them to a single digit.

For George we add the value of *G* (7), *L* (3), and *W* (5), which equals 15 and reduces to a 6.

> 1st initial is ____ Numeric value is ____.
>
> 2nd initial is ____ Numeric value is ____.
>
> 3rd initial is ____ Numeric value is ____.
>
>   Add. Reduce ____ = __ + __ = __ **Balance Number**

Use the numeric interpretations in Appendix A for the meaning of the Balance Number.

The First Vowel

The First Vowel shows your temperament or disposition; namely, how you predictably think, act, and behave. The First Vowel is your inner or soul vibration—it reveals character traits such as determination, will power, sensitivity, sociability, creativity, etc.

By looking at the First Vowel in a name you have a quick reference to that person. When a numerology chart is completed, this vibration shows very strongly throughout the chart. If a chart has not been made, the First Vowel can instantly describe the personality.

Vowel sounds have very important effects when being spoken. All long vowels are sonorous and positive in nature, with strong characteristic sounds accenting their vibrations. The short vowels cut the sound off immediately and are less obvious. With less expression to their sound, their vibrations are compressed and concise in nature.

Diphthongs express the vibrations of two vowel sounds at once if you slowly speak them and listen carefully. For example, in the name "Tom," a soft *a*, like in "ah," can be heard twice. In "Sam," the *a*, like in "as," sounds twice also. "Tony" has two *o*'s sounding, and in "Kim" the soft *i* is repeated. Notice that the word *twice* has the *i–e* combination sounding in its first vowel. These are the DUAL sounds used in pronouncing vowels, the diphthongs. Since diphthongs express two vowel vibrations, look for the interpretations of both vowels in the First Vowel interpretations text below.

(Note: Use the letter *y* as a vowel if there are no other vowels in the name or if the *y* sounds like a vowel.)

George has an *E* First Vowel.

Your FIRST VOWEL _____ (Place it on the worksheet on page 4)

FIRST VOWEL INTERPRETATIONS

A

The First Vowel *a* has the strength of the number 1. When it vibrates, it says "I AM, ME FIRST. I must do what the number 1 or the letter *A* tells me to do. I am the forceful letter. I lead, govern, create, invent. I use mental power to think out what I need to conquer any task. I know what must be done." This sounds like the long, or positive *A*. The short or concise *A* says, "I, too, am able to do the above, but not as long or as strong as the the positive *A*. I have pioneering spirit, yet do not take as long as the positive *A* to think about it. I do things faster, or in short order. I have to keep moving, for other things come up and I must be available to do them, too. I have the qualities of leadership, yet I appoint others to finish what I start. I need to do things as I want them done." These qualities are stronger if the short *A* is alone in a name. The diphthong says, "I have leadership and delegate it to others at the same time. I use two vibrations at once. Am I using the mental help from the *A*, the change of the *E*, the humanitarian vibrations of the *I*, the sense of responsibility of the *O*, or the pleasing personality and creativity of the *U*?" The average person will find that the vibrations of the *A* give strength, originality, ambition, intellectual capability, and creativity of some kind.

E

This changeable letter has many vibrations. It says, "I want to do as I see fit. I must not be tied down. I have many things to do at once. I have to change what I think can be changed. I must be working at something with variety. I need action. I have a lot to do in this life, and I want to do it all." This is the positive *E*, which has the strong vibrations of the 5. *E*'s must do. They have to be active and not in a rut. They need freedom at all costs, even if it means at the expense of their fellow workers or their family. *E*'s are not the kind to settle down. The short or concise *E*'s are the ones who do all of the above but in smaller amounts of time. They like short trips, want to be active, yet they enjoy quiet time to themselves to think about their next adventure. They are the ones who come and go often. They change residences and jobs often, and marry and divorce often. They are never quite satisfied with what they have and are always looking for a change. The dual or diphthong *E*'s have the changes of the short *E* in any combination with the strength of the *A*, which gives them the mental abilities to think out all possibilities; the vibrations of the 9 around the I, which gives them the ideas needed to help make the changes all humankind needs; the sense of responsibility of the 6 associated with the letter *O*, which gives them the stability they need to have a family and home; or the added creative abilities from the *U*. All *E*'s like the excitement of the unexpected. They insist upon change and their freedom to make the choices they see fit to make use of that change. They take on the vibrations of the 5. They are very interesting people and are invited to parties because they can liven things up.

I

The *I*'s have the ability to know what others need. They are the caring ones. They work well with others. They have kindness and understanding in their makeup. They are the humanitarians in this world because they do what they can to make it a better place to live in. The positive *I*'s are the very vibrant ones who need no introduction. They get to the point. They make themselves known to the world. They do not waste time. They have a lot to do and are always very busy. They often have creative talents that others can share in. When they make up their mind to do something, they do it without a second thought and no one can change their minds. They have a stubborn streak in them. The short *I*'s are the ones who have the capacity to work in many places with a variety of people. They are often found helping others in hospitals and charity wards, or doing charitable work or work of that nature. These are the soft-spoken humanitarians. They know what needs to be done and do it without comment or second thought. The dual *I*'s do things stronger if it is the *I* dominating, with more thought or mental help if it is in vibration with the *A*, with lots of changes for the better if the *E* is helping, with added responsibility if the *O* is in unison, and with pleasing personalities or creative abilities if the *U* is helping. These are the double-caring people. They have many duties. The average *I* is helpful, stable, unselfish, reliable, and caring.

O

The circle of the letter *O* means to hold within. This could have to do with emotions, which would give stress to the mental and physical body, or it could indicate domination of loved ones. When the *O* is vibrating it says, "I must do for those I love the most before I help others needing my assistance. I have to make my home and surroundings a place of beauty, contained in my circle again. I have to be responsible. I must do what I think is best for my family, friends, and those around me. I have to be working at something positive. I need to be needed. I must not be selfish. I want to be loved. I need a family and children to be the happiest. I care for the young and the old. I have compassion. I want to do what is best for humankind. I need responsible friends. I want to be known for the work I do. I need appreciation. I must at some time in my life be in the limelight." These are the positive *O*'s. They have the strength of the positive 6. The short *O*'s show compassion when they work with those in need. They have the beautiful surroundings of the 6 but in a small area. They vibrate to the shorter version of the positive *O*. They move about doing the little things for people that need to be done. They handle their responsibilities with care yet are able to ease themselves from the heavier burdens of the positive *O*. The dual vibrations of the diphthongs take the responsibility of the *O* doubly, or use the mental capabilities of an *A*, the changes of the *E*, the helping hand of the *I*, or the creative abilities of the *U* to aid in all they do. The *O*'s are unselfish, compassionate, responsible, sympathetic, and kind.

U

The positive *U*'s are the creative ones—they have all kinds of talents. They are good friends to many people. They like to show you what can be done with things in an artistic way. They are the decorators, the flower arrangers, the creators of beauty. They are softspoken, have many things to say, and know what to say when needed. They have the ability to work well with most people, children being their favorite. They love to paint, write, sing, debate, lecture, or act. They show positive traits when working with people. They must be given their own time in which to do their creations. They have many friends because they are pleasing people. They want to be liked and do what they can to please all. The short *U* sound gives this person many talents to use, and they do use them. They know what is needed when they are asked to work on projects of art, advertising, decorating, or other things that need to be organized for eye appeal. They have a strong desire for variety in what they do, and they complete projects in the smallest time possible so that there is time left for more activities. The diphthong nature of the *U* gives duality or double strength to the talents or creations of this person, while the *A* could add intellectual abilities, the *E* give changes, the *I* give compassion or put a finishing touch on a project, and the *O* could add responsibility. The *U* vibrates pleasing personalities, friends, creativity, inventions, intuition, hobbies, and the ability to work with and use words in many ways.

Y

The *Y*'s always crave the knowledge needed to satisfy their curiosity. They are the silent types. All *Y*'s have the ability to reason, think, and delve into the mysteries of life. They look to the ends of the Earth if they want to know the truth or get the proof of something they do not know or understand. They are the scientists, the teachers, the detail gatherers, or the inventors. They have the need to know. This search for knowledge could also involve in-depth study of different religions. When the strong 7 is vibrating it says, "I need to be alone to do my own thing. I want friends, yet I want only a few well-chosen, close acquaintances. I must not be disturbed unless I want to be. I will spread my information among all when I write or lecture, or when asked about subjects that I am interested in and know about. I have the ability to speak well in public when I know the subject. I do not carry on private conversations if I am bored." The short *Y* vibrates to shorter versions of the above. They are easily bored and like to do things on a smaller scale. They have many opportunities and take advantage of all, changing many jobs, studies, or other things of interest. The dual *Y* will have the feelings of the letter it sounds most like. Most are the changes of the *E*. All *Y*'s are kindly people when you get to know them. Outwardly they are quiet, hard to understand, and show a variety of interests. They are nature lovers. Most are intelligent, sensitive, honest, and reserved.

Achievement

This indicates something that must be accomplished in life, a mission. Until this Achievement is met, understood, and accepted, the resulting tension could bring out the negative vibrations of the number.

The Achievement number is found by adding the month of birth digit to the day of birth digit and reducing to a single digit—our familiar Birth digit (B.D.).

George's Achievement number is 4.

> Your ACHIEVEMENT number _____ (the Birth digit).

Use the numeric value meanings from Appendix A for the explanation.

Capstone

This is the manner in which you react to everyday life. The Capstone is the *last letter* in the first name. The first name is the attracting and outgoing vibrations in life. The Capstone is the completion. Use the letter only, not the numeric value.

George's Capstone is *E.*

> The last letter of your first name _____ = **Capstone.**

Use the letter meanings in Appendix B for the explanation.

Keystone

If the first name has an odd number of letters, the middle letter is the Keystone and it vibrates more individual characteristics of the personality. If the first name has an even amount of letters (like George), there is no Keystone. In the name "Susan" the third letter, or the *S*, is the Keystone.

> The middle letter of the first name _____ = **Keystone.**

Use the following text for interpretation.

KEYSTONE INTERPRETATIONS

A   Intellectual skills, mental powers.
B   Compassionate, gentle, helpful.
C   Creative abilities and mentalities.
D   Likes recognition, may need urging.
E   Logical, analytical, likes research.
F   Not easily convinced, firm in opinion.
G   Determined, may be aloof.
H   Capable of achievement in business.
I   Inspirational speaker, strong personal opinions.
J   Systematic, orderly, needs money to be happy.
K   Teaches and aids others.
L   Reasoning power, loves justice.
M   Hard worker, always active.
N   Versatile, adaptable.
O   Willful, self-enclosed.
P   Meditative, understands unseen things, likes to be alone.
Q   Executive ability, assumes responsibility.
R   Selfless, inspires confidence in others.
S   Very emotional, independent, cunning.
T   Inventive, gentle, could be highstrung.
U   Conservative, careful of detail, does not like advice.
V   Intuitive, capable, organizer, builder, discreet.
W   Versatile, strong belief in justice, nature lover.
X   Artistic, talented, very considerate, gallant.
Y   Compassionate, perceptive, underestimates self.
Z   Can organize and promote, understanding, visionary.

Name Characteristic

This is an added bit of information that your name could be vibrating. It is derived from the number of letters in a full name—not the numeric values, just how many letters make up the name. Remember that the higher the number that you start out with before you reduce to a single digit, the more powerful the vibrations will be.

George Lester Whiteside has 21 letters in his name. The 2 + 1 equals a 3 Name Characteristic. He could be very creative or excel in other talents such as writing or speaking.

Number of letters in full name ____ = __ + __ = __ **Name Characteristic.**

NAME CHARACTERISTIC INTERPRETATIONS

1   One-track mind. Original. Sometimes abrupt.
2   Orderly, likes detail. May be shy or in a shell.
3   Expressive or creative talents. Some may need encouragement.
4   Good worker, cautious. Confront your problems.
5   Likes variety, very changeable. Needs stability.
6   Creates beautiful surroundings. Often too domineering.
7   Ability to specialize. Dignity could be easily injured.
8   Has the ability to mediate, arbitrate. Needs to use sound judgment.
9   Pleasing personality. Could be temperamental at times.
11 Visionary inspiration, spiritual-minded. Often shy.
22 Master mind, hard worker. Could become a workaholic.

Now let's look back a bit. The Cornerstone, Key, and Capstone perform in connection with each other. The Cornerstone is the foundation life is built on, the Key is the characteristic style in which life is lived, and the Capstone is the outcome of activities or undertakings. All use the first name some way or other. A pyramid form could be used to place the Cornerstone at the bottom left, the Key at the bottom right, and the Capstone on top. This shows the style of life's existence. Your first name is your special name, your vibration. Most people are called by it more than by their full name. It vibrates the most in your life because of this. Your name is used in numerology more than your birth date, but it does not mean that it is the most important vibration.

Other vibrations have been shown throughout this workbook. We kept some to a minimum because other books go into detail on them.

We have some very important vibrations, vibrations that affect our lives every day, to work out in the rest of this book. When you learn how to figure all of these you will know the main structure of basic numerology.

We will start next with the Reality Number, go on to the Planes of Expression, and the Excursion, or Transits. Then comes additional information and a summary. By then you should be able to do anyone's numerology chart.

Reality Number
(Life Number, Ultimate Goal, Power Number)

Consider the Reality Number to be one of the most important numbers in a person's life. When you look into this number you will see what your life was planned for. If you know the plan and try to live up to its meaning your life will be meaningful, useful, and happy. Even if this number is not known, it has an influence that a person could be entirely unaware of, something that makes them wonder why they chose to do this or that in their life. You will find that you will recognize some of your likes and dislikes. Vibrations are being felt all through the life. If this number is lived up to, there will be no wasted, useless days in your life and retirement will be active and not sedentary. It is the clue to your being and to your greatest successes because it gives you a life purpose.

Put this prominent number in its place early enough in life so that it becomes a part of your reality. Knowing what it vibrates in your life will make life more meaningful.

Only a handful of people vibrate to the true vibrations of the Master Number of 11 and 22 when it is in this position. Those few who do will recognize it as their calling. So reduce even the Master Numbers to the 11/2 or the 22/4 combination.

The Reality Number is found by adding the Path of Life digit (birth date) to the Expression digit (full name) and reducing to a single number. The explanations for the Reality Number are listed below.

When we add George's Path of Life 7 to his Expression's 4 we get a Reality Number of 11/2.

Fill in the blanks below and place the digit on the worksheet on page 4.

Path of Life digit ___

Expression digit   + ___

Total and reduce   = __ + __ = __ REALITY NUMBER.

REALITY NUMBER INTEPRETATIONS

1

A very independent person. Creative, talented, original. Their ambition and strongly expressed opinions often make them leaders and directors. But they should guard against becoming dictatorial because they can be very domineering, overbearing, and demanding. They prefer to do their own thing and use their own ideas, since they dislike having others tell them what to do. If they ask advice from others, they never use it because they are only in tune to their own strong convictions. They are capable of carrying out large-scale plans. They must be busy. They like to carry through with their own plans, usually accomplishing what they have set out to do. They take prompt action when an idea or plan is clearly set in their mind. They usually are the business leaders, directors, executives, inventors, engineers, department heads, designers, or in any position in which originality and leadership is essential. They are the pioneers. Being very stubborn and opinionated could cause problems with associates. All negative vibrations of this number should be corrected, because they could make this 1 very unpopular. Their ego or conceit brings resentment and jealousy. They must learn to think of others. Their success comes through themselves, by using their own creativity.

2

These popular and pleasant people are the peacemakers, arbitrators, and diplomats. Some are inclined to religious or spiritual work and teachings. The 2's should work with groups for greatest success in life. They could be advisers or consultants. Their interest in art, music, libraries, and museums could give them many opportunities and much pleasure. They should pursue their talents, or they will regret it later in life. The number 2 people could be musicians, orators, arbitrators, diplomats, ministers, ambassadors, spiritual healers, or anything having to do with medicine; accountants, bankers, financiers—anything to do with money; secretaries, statisticians, electricians or radio workers. Their success comes through association with others. Their key word is *cooperation*. Partnerships could give them trouble in the first half of their life. They need love, sympathy, tenderness, and patience. These are the qualities they give to others while trying to do the right thing to please and share. They are peacemakers and will fight for that peace if absolutely necessary. They have psychic and intuitive powers, which should not be misused. The negative 2 could be a person with an inferiority complex; someone who is extremely shy, who dreads meeting people, and who tries to stay away from others' opinions. Nervousness and tension could result if the negative attitudes are not overcome. They should avoid becoming doormats.

3

Self-expression is the key word because 3's find their opportunities in writing, speaking, or acting. They are the imaginative, the artistic, the creative people. Inhibition in early life—whether due to health or self-consciousness—could mean an unsuccessful life. If this can be overcome they are cheerful, optimistic and successful. They are very self-determined, generous to a fault, sensitive, agreeable, obliging, often impatient with the practical but very practical with detail. Because they are very self-conscious, criticism could be taken in the wrong sense, causing them to end a career. Inside they have a strong feeling of self-importance, and if this is used positively it could help them reach their goals. They love the spotlight. They like to have their own way, but may show indifference at times, even refusing to do what does not please them. They are good lecturers, writers, composers, singers, entertainers, or decorators. Sometimes they are in the stock market, real estate, commercial or mechanical arts, armed forces, boxing (they love to fight or give a sharp comeback), or in public life. Could be mediumistic. They like music (especially opera), color and beauty, and make lasting friends. Negative vibrations could indicate the oversensitive, self-conscious, self-important, self-determined, impatient, worrier, or extravagant person. Success can be obtained if their talents are not scattered.

4

These are the foundation makers, the practical workers. They bring dreams to life. They must make a usable or practical foundation upon which to build their ideas and goals. This could be in the scientific, religious, artistic, or business world. Their persistent nature helps them to put their deep inner ideas into form. They are hard workers, sometimes even workaholics, keeping their nose to the grindstone. Time is very important in whatever they plan or build. Their patience and steadfastness bring far greater results than sudden impulses and haste, which could be their undoing. They learn by their own mistakes. The easy paths of life are not for them. They are exact and patient in detail because the practical side controls their movement. They are sympathetic, honest, kind, have strong principles, are full of energy, and have the reasoning power to understand all the facts. Family ties often hold them down. To be happy they need to be in a life that they created through their own efforts. They are not the social mixers, instead preferring a few good friends with similar interests. Usually these people are in business for themselves or are the regulators, administrators, or managers, for they like to give the orders. Some are shopkeepers, the fixers and suppliers for our needs in daily life. The negative side exhibits strict authoritarianism, conceit, dominance, or exactingness. If held down they are moody, resentful, and narrow. To succeed in life they must build with their own ideas and their own constructive plans.

5

These are the multifaceted, progressive, independent spirits of the world. They love variety. They are enthusiastic, resourceful, clever, versatile, imaginative, curious, witty, energetic, and magnetic. They are able to look ahead and grab the opportunities while others are just thinking about them. Their opportunities come through change and new ideas, but they should be cautioned that change should be made only after they have perfected what they have been doing, acquiring some measure of skill in their work. They should remember all the lessons from their mental, emotional, and spiritual experiences, extracting the net worth of each and every one. Public activities are of interest to them. Opportunities come as reporters, writers, lawyers, politicians, metaphysicians, entertainers; or in sports, advertising, commercial art, travel, fashion, promotion, speculation (not gambling), counseling, research, or through scientific study. A warning: they should *not* scatter their energies or have too many irons in the fire, because justice will not be done to any of their projects. The negative are restless, energy scatterers, impatient, critical, eccentric, boastful, or indifferent; they fail to give credit where it is due and are destructive because of discontentment. Their reality comes through progressive changes in public, worldly, or business activities. They need an active life with lots of changes and travel. They find stimulation through people. They attract the opposite sex and have many unconventional, worldly experiences.

6

The humanitarian—consideration of and service to others are their duty and responsibility. These are the family-minded people. Their home and relatives mean a lot to them. Home and family is where they look for approval, sympathy, and love. They are peace seekers, for they need harmony in order to do their best. They are romantic, affectionate, idealistic, honest, just, truthful, and have strong principles. Their sense of duty and service often causes them to make extreme sacrifices, sometimes senselessly, for some person or ideal. They like to be doing worthwhile, useful things. They do not like to be challenged about their ideals or methods and can be very unreasonable and stubborn, and they have a personal side to them that hides any imperfections of their own or their loved ones. If they cannot do what they want to do, they do nothing at all. They can be outspoken and blunt, sometimes telling people what is wrong with them, but are unable to take their own medicine. They overcome their faults through sympathy, not criticism. They are the helping hand when trouble comes to others. They are happiest when serving humanity. Many marry later in life. They are very artistic, and like music, gardening, and interior decorating. They could be singers, actors, teachers, doctors, nurses, poets, engineers, ranchers, lawyers, landscapers, horticulturists, miners, potters, commercial artists, painters, chefs, or furniture makers or upholsterers. This benevolent number also succeeds through welfare work, charitable institutions, hospitals, or service-related occupations. Boats and ships attract these people. The negative are overbearing, domineering, interfering, irresponsible, stubborn, and argumentative. Their success comes as they do more for others.

7

Sevens are reserved and thoughtful—the seekers of wisom and understanding. They are often misunderstood because they are the silent types and like their privacy—the world thinks they are in a shell. When they want to open up, they can be very good speakers, because they have the knowledge to expound on any subject that interests them. They search for the inner answers to all the mysteries in life. They are the researchers, thinkers, developers, scientists, dreamers, skeptics, inventors, and mystics. They are all looking for the unseen, cold, hard, true facts, the undiscovered. When they relate to others, they are charming, good-natured, convincing, and have a pleasing personality. Knowledge is foremost to them. They would rather read than anything else; but if they keep their noses in the books too much they could become dull and lose contact with the outside world, which could cause them to lose some opportunities. Due to their attitude and nature, marriage is sometimes a problem to them. They love a stylish, well-furnished home, and expect to be the head of the household. Their friends are selected carefully, since they dislike having too many people around at the same time. Their opportunities could come through some special line of work. They are the historians, chemists, technicians, accountants, lawyers, surgeons, statisticians, insurance agents, laboratory workers, detectives, secret service agents, criminologists, and are involved in anything having to do with the spiritual world. Because they work well with their hands, they often become artists of all types and talents, or musicians. If their ability and knowledge is put to good use, they can become famous by presenting the world with some innovative idea. The negative could be impatient, secretive, nervous, overcritical, confused, crafty, or alcoholic. They could also be rebellious or insurgent.

8

Most think the 8 is the money number, but it is the way the 8's manage their money that is important here. If they manage it wisely they will have no problems, but if they spend it extravagantly they will have lost the meaning of their number. Eight is a material achievement number, but only to those who do not put it first in their lives. Desire for wealth and personal power can bring loss of that very thing. The 8's must learn to balance the spiritual and the material, because when they reach this balance they will accomplish their purpose with just rewards. These are the counselors, the analysts, and researchers who supervise and direct the affairs of others. They need strong character and leadership capabilities. Real estate and other types of property may be under their supervision. These are the natural psychologists and philosophers, since they can look into life as it really is. In this way they can help others to understand themselves. The 8's are on a continually balancing scale, and if their life has a worthwhile purpose all will be well, but if the scale tips in the direction of the selfish, there will be a loss that will be hard to regain. They could succeed as writers, travel agents, instructors, supervisors, coaches, athletes, explorers, managers, superintendents, civil engineers, insurance agents, real estate agents, architects, professional artists, hotel or resort owners, publishers, statisticians, or business executives. They love nature and have a way with animals. If they live up to their purpose they can become great masters and mystics, with the whole world looking to them for understanding. The negative are ambitious, materialistic, selfish, wasteful, miserly, unreliable, thoughtless, or want personal power.

9

To be compassionate and selfless is the goal of the number 9. They must give up the personal and become the impersonal. They will learn that to succeed they must give up the material and look to the spiritual laws that are compelling them to the higher planes of awareness. Their affairs are conducted in large circles protected by cosmic energy. They have the power, kindness, sympathy, and generosity to help the weak, old, and the poor by lighting up their lives and showing them warmth and understanding. But if they try to turn that light upon themselves for personal gain it could backfire and destroy their own lives and power. When their Soul Growth is obtained they become the chosen people of the earth. They are idealistic, romantic, and emotional, and fall deeply in love. Any romance can end very quickly if that love does not stand up to their ideals. Some 9's, being shy and unassertive, often need a hand until they realize that they have the power to lure the good and perfect gifts through service and love. Nines are difficult to change and reform when they have developed the wrong habits, but they are capable of reaching the highest goals in life when they overcome their faults. They have both sides of life shown to them from early life on, and it is up to them to take the correct road. They have the power that none of the other numbers do—to rise from the bottom and reach the highest goal in life. They like beauty, are charming and creative, and have the ability to attract the comforts in life. They are well suited to be teachers, writers, actors, surgeons, painters, designers, lawyers, architects, speakers, ministers, philanthropists, cabinetmakers, upholsterers, or any occupations involving creation of beautiful things. They should rise above petty interests, cultivate a universal outlook, and know that service to humankind does have rewards. The negative could be over emotional, impractical, unkind, bitter, selfish, or unstable.

11

This intriguing and inspirational number will always indicate someone in the limelight. Elevens must work for the benefit of all. They have very strong psychic abilities, and some become mediums, preachers, or other kinds of religious leaders. They must live a pure life to accomplish their purpose in life. They must be honest, faithful to God, and share what they know to be the truth. What these people know comes from the ancients—they are the Old Souls who have vast knowledge.They give all they can to enlighten others. Some may find this number hard to live up to, so check the meaning of the 2.

22

Here again we have the master builders. These are the people who create on a large scale, usually for all humankind. These are the brilliant-minded, the most inventive, the scientific. They are the specialists in any field that requires hard work, either mental or physical. They embody the stronger vibrations of the 4. When these people act, they do so because it has been well thought out and their plans have been put in order. They know it will work. Bridges, skyscrapers, or shopping centers are just a few examples of their work. Many specialize in medicine or in other fields that benefit humankind. If this number is too hard to live up to, go to the 4.

Planes of Expression

We use all the letters in the full name to express ourselves. The Planes of Expression is a chart which tells how each letter in our name is helping to bring about this expression.

There are four Planes by which we can describe ourselves: the Mental, the Physical, the Emotional, and the Intuitive. They are each equal in value; one is not more favorable than another. These Planes can tell us about our temperaments—whether we are practical or dependable, for example—and it can help determine what kind of job we are best suited for. In other words it points out our assets and liabilities, our pluses or minuses. It shows where we have the most knowledge and ability. A shortage on one Plane does not mean that the person is completely lacking in that quality, because it could be vibrating in one of the major numbers elsewhere.

Mental Plane: These are the ones that think things out. They test with their minds. They are the leaders, the scientists, the inventors, the heads of large businesses. They are the writers of serious or technical works. They have strong reasoning power and they deal with the facts.

Physical Plane: These are the practical ones. They use their energies on the real, the here and now. They have endurance, are systematic, and have positive opinions. They use physical power, not mental. They are the hard workers, the builders, the craftspeople.

Emotional Plane: These are the ones with feelings, imagination, sentiment. They are creative, having originality and inspiration. They are guided by their emotions. They care little for facts or analysis. They are artistic.

Intuitive Plane: These are the intuitive ones. They are psychically inclined; their inner voices help them, and ideas come quickly. They are interested in spiritual matters and seek knowledge and inspiration.

The first word of all the letter meanings in the Alphabet Values and Meanings text in Appendix B indicates the appropriate Plane for each letter.

THE THREE SUBDIVISIONS

Each plane is further divided into three subdivisions: Inspired or Creative, Dual or Vacillating, and Balanced or Grounded.

Inspired or Creative letters: the initiators, instigators, or creators; the pioneers, the inventors.

Dual or Vacillating letters: those wavering indecisively from one course of action or opinion to another.

Balanced or Grounded: the steadfast ones; have both feet on the ground, self-assured, established.

Note: there are no Balanced or Grounded letters on the Emotional Plane. You cannot be emotional and still be grounded or balanced.

The following Planes of Expression Table shows the proper placement of each letter of the alphabet.

PLACEMENT TABLE OF THE PLANES OF EXPRESSION

	Mental	Physical	Emotional	Intuitive	Totals
Inspired Creative	A	E	O R I Z	K	7
Dual Vacillating	H J N P	W	B S T X	F Q U Y	13
Balanced Grounded	G L	D M		C V	6
Totals	7	4	8	7	26

Now refer to the table for George below as an example.

TABLE OF THE PLANES OF EXPRESSION

	Mental	Physical	Emotional	Intuitive	Totals
Inspired Creative		E E E E E E	O R R I I		11
Dual Vacillating	H	W	S T T S		6
Balanced Grounded	G G L	D			4
Totals	4	8	9		21

Use the following chart to find your own Planes of Expression. Place each and every letter of the full name in the appropriate box (even those repeated go in as many times as they are in the name), then add the letters in the boxes both vertically and horizontally. Place the totals in the appropriate boxes. They should add up to the number of letters in the full name (not the numeric value, just how many letters).

PLANES OF EXPRESSION

	Mental	Physical	Emotional	Intuitive	Totals
Inspired Creative					
Dual Vacillating					
Balanced Grounded					
Totals					

To interpret what your name vibrates, look down each row and column and evaluate the total of the letters. Those letters appearing with the highest frequency will have the strongest vibrations; those appearing the lowest number of times will have a weaker influence; and those that are missing indicate that their qualities are unimportant in your makeup. Appendix B gives the meanings for each letter. When you use this table you will be able to find out how you react to certain situations, jobs, or events. It will let you know why you are vibrating toward a certain kind of situation. A Planes of Expression chart can show why some become scientists and others artists, why some are confused in one job and do well in another, why some use brain while others use brawn.

The Excursion
(Table of Events, Immediate Period)

Using the letters, their numeric values in a name, and the Personal and Universal Year digits, this chart is used to figure the past, present, and future of the person the name represents. It could tell you why things are happening, give highlights in life, and focus upon turning points. It helps show you the transit or movement that each letter makes throughout a lifetime.

A *transit* means the letter is moving through life, sending out vibrations for the number of years equal to its numeric value. Like the transit of planets in astrology, letter transits start at birth and move in cycles of varying duration. The *A* vibrates for one year, the *B* vibrates for two years, the *C* for three years, etc. (For a complete breakdown of alphabet values, see Appendix B.) Unlike the Personal Year and Universal Year, which have their influence from January 1st to December 31st, the vibrations of the letters are in effect from birthday to birthday.

The following is a sample Excursion chart using a fictitious name and birth date.

Name and Birth Date: J o h n   P a u l   J o n e s   Jan. 1, 1901
Numeric Values: 1 6 8 5   7 1 3 3   1 6 5 5 1   1   1   11/2

AGE	TRANSIT			LETTER VALUE			ESSENCE	P.Y.	U.Y.	YEAR
	F	M	L	F	M	L				
0-1	J	P	J	1	7	1	= 9	4	11/2	1901
1-2	O	P	O	6	7	6	= 1	5	3	1902
3	O	P	O	6	7	6	= 1	6	4	1903
4	O	P	O	6	7	6	= 1	7	5	1904
5	O	P	O	6	7	6	= 1	8	6	1905
6	O	P	O	6	7	6	= 1	9	7	1906
7	O	P	O	6	7	6	= 1	1	8	1907
8	H	A	N	8	1	5	= 5	2	9	1908
9	H	U	N	8	3	5	= 7	3	1	1909
Etc.										

The first vertical column is for the AGE. (Note: the year of birth to the first birthday is the number 1 year, even though age 1 has not been reached.)

The TRANSIT portion of the chart uses three separate columns for the letters in the full name. The first-name letters are placed under column *F*, the middle-name letters under column *M*, and the last-name letters under column *L*. In the first name "John," the letter *J* is equal to 1, so it is written in the first colum for one year; the *O* is equal to 6, so it is written down the column for the next six years; the *H* (8) is used for the next eight years; the *N* (5) for the next five years, then *J* (1) would be repeated for one year, starting the cycle over again.

Each name section has the duration of the total value of that part of the name. "John" fully cycles in 20 years, "Paul" cycles in 14 years, and "Jones" has a cycle of 18 years. At the end of each cycle, each name section starts over, repeating again and again. Shorter names transit to their fullest faster than long names or names with high letter values.

The LETTER VALUE section is also divided into three columns, corresponding to the numeric values of the first, middle, and last name letters.

The ESSENCE, or total value of the three letters reduced to a single digit, belongs in the next column.

The P.Y. and U.Y. columns are for the Personal Year and Universal Year digits, and the year represented goes in the YEAR column.

This chart can be filled out to cover the dates in question for any personal event by placing the ages that you wish to know about down the first column; but it is easier, especially for a beginner, to start with the birth year and work up to the present so that mistakes will be kept to a minimum. If you know what letter is vibrating during a certain year you can make partial charts.

Now it's your turn. Fill in the chart below.

Using the alphabet values chart in Appendix B, figure out the letter transits for the name you are working with and place them in their appropriate columns in the Transit section across from the corresponding ages. (Remember that from birth to the first birthday is the number 1 age; letters start their transiting vibrations at birth.)

Next fill in the three Letter Value columns with the digits that correspond to the letters in the Transit section. If working with the Master Letters *K* or *V*, reduce them to single digits for this chart.

Now add the letter values together for each age line, reduce to a single digit (there is room to pencil in the figuring if needed), and place that number in the Essence column. (If the Master Numbers 11 or 22 make up the Essence total, they will be written as an 11/2 or a 22/4. Read both 11=2 and the 2, or the 22=4 and the 4, for interpretations in the text that follows.)

Figure the Personal Year and Universal Year digits and put them in their columns in line with the matching year. Complete the entire chart to cover the dates you want to know about.

EXCURSION CHART

AGE	TRANSIT			LETTER VALUE			ESSENCE	P.Y.	U.Y.	YEAR
	F	M	L	F	M	L				
							=			
							=			
							=			
							=			
							=			
							=			
							=			
							=			
							=			
							=			
							=			
							=			
							=			
							=			
							=			
							=			
							=			
							=			
							=			
							=			
							=			
							=			
							=			

When you have finished the first line across the chart you can use a shortcut for the age, Personal Year, Universal Year, and the year on all of the next lines. Once you have figured out the first-line digits for these columns you just add 1 to each digit for the next line all the way down the chart, checking for Master Numbers in the P.Y. and U.Y. columns. If you are using the same digits that you have already figured elsewhere in a chart, you can transfer the ones needed to this or any other chart or table (the Path of Life digit is always the Personal Year digit for the year of birth for example.)

Now you are ready to read the chart. Compare the Essence to the Personal Year and Universal Year digits, taking into consideration the letters used in the Transit section. Remember that the Essence is in effect from birthday to birthday and that the Personal and Universal Years run from January 1st to December 31st of each year. In other words, the Essence can overlap into another year up to the next birthday. Be sure you check this when you are comparing the vibrations of the letters and the Essence with the years. Also check to see if any of the digits match another digit. Matching numbers can soften vibrations, making things easier to manage; others give a conflicting effect to make us put effort into our lives.

In addition, it is very important that you check and compare other numbers in the chart, especially the principal ones, to see which digits may be in effect at the same time as the Essence.

EXCURSION INTERPRETATIONS

Listed here are the meanings of the Essence numbers and the transits of the letters in the full name.

In the first section the single-digit meanings of the Essence are given first, followed by number combinations that could be giving additional messages. Always take into account the numbers and the letters used to find the single digit for the Essence, because these may have hidden background vibrations.

The second section gives the key vibrations of the letter transits for further insight into the character of each letter.

For more complete interpretations of each letter, you may want to refer to the alphabet meaning text in Appendix B.

1

All the vibrations of the 1. This could mean new beginnings or a change of some sort. Individuality, ambition, initiative, new directions, or adding something new to established enterprises.

10=1 This is a stronger vibration of the 1. It carries all of the definitions of the 1 but with added strength.

19=1 Understanding and unselfishness of the 9. A time to learn the vibrations of the humanitarian. This could cause a struggle between the self (1) and a need to be unselfish.

28=1 This strong 1 vibration derives from the cooperation with others (2) and from the good management ability (8) needed to start projects that benefit many.

2

Marriage or divorce, partnerships or associations, are the vibrations here. A time for opportunity, emotions, and assistance to or from others. Cooperation is needed on your part in all things. Take care of the little things to the best of your ability. Have patience in all you do.

11=2 Inner or spiritual peace is needed to help you through the changes and hurts that can come in this period. There could be sudden and unexpected separations in marriage or partnerships causing great emotional upsets. A willingness to cooperate and share is your top priority now.

20=2 Stronger vibrations of all of the 2. This is the time to be the helping hand, or to use the help offered. When a stronger number vibrates, it must be noted that more power is behind the meanings.

3

A pleasant time now. A time for self-improvement and self-advancement. A time for personal expression linked with career advancement. Enjoy children and old friends, and make new friends. Keep busy with some useful interest. This is not the time to scatter your energies or financial resources. Nor is it a time for emotions. Be generous but always businesslike.

12=3 When the 1 adds the vibration of new beginnings, and the 2 gives its cooperation to the creations of the 3, larger projects are worked on with the intention of benefiting humankind. This could be scientific.

21=3 The time to take into account others who need or offer a helping hand (2). This help comes from or is given to the self (1).

4

A time to get things done in an orderly manner. Now is the time to build a new home or business. Put forth effort, be practical, use good judgment in all things, and good results will follow. Relatives (in-laws) make demands. Guard your health.

13=4 This 1 adds a beginning or individual ambition to the creations or inventions (3) needed to build or put in order.

22=4 This is a sensitive time. Quarrels and disagreements could cause loss. A willingness to share and attention to these matters are needed now. Don't run away—face up to the situation. This will better the relationship. Stress can cause illness. This is the time to stop and get a better understanding of yourself and others.

5

Changes of all kinds, both expected and unexpected, can happen now. It could be new places, new jobs, or new people. Try not to scatter your energies by having too many things going on at one time. Impatience can cause legal conflicts. This is a time to advance or get free from past conditions.

14=5 Avoid hasty action (4). Trouble can be overcome by sticking to the letter of the law (1 self).

23=5 Travels. Take others into consideration (2). Unusual lines of work could be started now (3).

6

This is the time for home, family, love, and marriage. A time for unselfish aid to humankind, which in turn can bring gains to you. Children could be a problem at this time. Try to live up to your responsibilities without being domineering, thoughtless, selfish, or possessive. This is a time of marrige or divorce if there is strife. Financial gain or inheritance are a possibility under this number. Unselfish deeds and service to humankind are rewarded with social recognition, popularity, and good standing in the community.

15=6 Could be a problem with the opposite sex. (1) self-will, (5) freedom.

24=6 More cooperation (2) and good management (4).

7

A time to delve deeper into the unanswered or the unknown. A time to add to your talents. A time for deep thought. Ask yourself if you understand the purpose and objective reality of your being, or what life is all about. Now is the time to study the spiritual or metaphysical world. You may find yourself involved in research or scientific investigation. This is the best period to add to your education in any area. This is not the best time for marriage, unless the intelligence and interest levels are the same. A 7 Essence indicates that care must be taken regarding health concerns.

16=7   This denotes selfless (1) aid to humanity (6). Could be the time to write that book or give that lecture for the benefit of others.

26=7   Use the help from others (2) to make the changes (5) needed in your work or your life.

8

You should be able to achieve what you have set out to do, but it may involve a lot of effort and responsibility. You may find yourself buying or selling property, managing a business or personal affairs, or getting involved in civic or governmental matters in a large way. Now is the time for working with groups of people. Good judgment is necessary in all your money dealings, because expenses can be high during an 8. Money comes and goes and needs proper management.

17=8   The individuality of the 1, together with the knowledge of the 7, gives the self the control and know-how to manage the responsibilities in their life.

26=8   The double helping hands of the 2 and the 6 say it is time to work with others. They have qualities that you may need to accomplish your goals.

9

Big opportunities arise through humanitarian efforts. Legal problems may come through dishonesty. Lawsuits could take a long time to settle, but honesty, truth, and justice usually prevail. The 9 Essence gives unlimited opportunities in business, literary, creative, educational or religious lines. The emotions and deep feelings of the 9 could make this an unhappy time, but if a positive attitude is maintained, there is much to gain. A 9 usually has some kind of loss. If it is money, more will come to replace it. It may be a job, a home, or even through a love lost, a divorce, a separation or death. Whatever the loss for a 9, there will always be a replacement somewhere, so don't let the loss get you down. Pick up the pieces and go on to new and better opportunities. Watch your health. This is the time to help, counsel, and advise others. Use caution to avoid accidents.

18=9   The vibrations of the self (1) and the management of the (8) give this 9 the ability to take hold of all projects and finish them with ease.

27=9   The cooperation from the 2 mixed with the knowledge or seeking action of the 7 helps this 9 to find solutions needed to put the finishing touch on enterprises.

KEY LETTER VIBRATIONS

A – J – S

Transit duration: one year. These letters always indicate a time to start something new. Use your original ideas and your initiative.

B – K – T

Transit duration: two years. This period will always involve others. Watch emotions and health. This could be a time for marriage or divorce, companionship or partnership.

C – L – U

Transit duration: three years. This will always be a time for personal expression through creative abilities.

D – M – V

Transit duration: four years. This transit will always involve working for the future. This is the time to be practical, orderly, and use good management.

E – N – W

Transit duration: five years. This time will always be active with lots of changes. With added stability this could be a very progressive period.

F – O – X

Transit duration: six years. This transit will always involve the home and community. This is the time for responsibilities to family and others.

G – P – Y

Transit duration: seven years. These letters always indicate a search for knowledge. This is a time for mental pursuits.

H – Q – Z

Transit duration: eight years. Management of personal or business concerns will be emphasized during this period. If properly managed, this is a time for achievement or advancement.

I – R

Transit duration: nine years. This transit will involve understanding the needs of others. A loss here brings something better in replacement. Always use caution during a 9 so that others do not abuse your kindness.

Miscellaneous Information

The following pages will give added information on how to use numbers in other ways that may or may not pertain to a numerology chart date or name. This will be added information that we feel you would like to know about. It may be helpful or useful in some instances and only informational in others.

INTROVERT AND EXTROVERT NUMBERS

In some books these are called the Great With-In and the Great With-Out.

Introvert numbers are the odd numbers: 1, 3, 5, 7, 9, 11. They represent the inspirational, the artistic, the shy, the dreamers. They are emotional, spiritual, and have idealistic viewpoints. They stand up for their own rights and want to accomplish all on their own. They dislike crowds but need people for success.

Extrovert numbers are the even numbers: 2, 4, 6, 8, 22. These numbers fabricate, organize, structure, or create in form. They prefer the company of other people, and they give others help when needed. They bring action, fun, and enjoyment into our lives. They manage and direct.

Dual numbers are 1, 6, 22. They are inspirational artists with-in, but capable of expression in form with-out.

Additional classification of the numbers and letters

1–5–7   They get what they go after. They activate things.

2–4–8   They get things done. The managers and directors. They work for their money.

3–6–9   They believe the best is there for their taking. They need help from others to succeed. They have the ability to make big money.

			THE ONE			THE MANY				THE ALL	
1	2	3	4	5	6	7		8	9	11	22
A	B	C	D	E	F	G		H	I	K	V
J		L	M	N	O	P		Q	R		
S	T	U		W	X	Y		Z			

The keyword for the one is *mine;* for the many, *ours;* and for the all, *yours.* The 7 is a bridge between the Many and the All but is still connected to the Many world of form by its system and concept.

You will find that we are a combination of the above classifications. Some of these assessments contradict the general meaning of a few of the numbers. There should not be competition between them, because when they are understood and put to good use they help strengthen the main numbers in the chart. This just might be the vibration that was lacking to help reach a goal or to read a chart correctly.

KARMIC NUMBERS

Many people do not believe in karma and past lives, but for those who do, I put in the paragraph below so that they will know how to find them.

The Karmic Number is an unpaid dept from past lives for things that were put to wrong or improper use. Look at the SUBTOTALS in the birth date, Soul Urge, Expression, and Quiet Self. The numbers are 13 (didn't apply self to work, a fear of death); 14 (too much personal freedom, sex); 16 (self-centered life, illicit love affairs); and 19 (misuse of power, must pay back for something taken).

There are many numerology books that explain karma in more detail for those who want to know more.

COLOR

When I first started this book I didn't have much information on color, so I was going to state that it would be up to the student to use their own judgment. But with the help of my guides, we wrote the following:

Each color vibrates to a different number.

The color red.. is number 1.
The color orange....................................... is number 2.
The color yellow .... is number 3.
The color green.. is number 4.
The color blue... is number 5.
The color purple .... is number 6.
The color black... is number 7.
The color gray... is number 8.
The color white .... is number 9.

Color vibrates all around us, and you can feel the effects of those vibrations. Color affects the way we respond to everyday living. We feel better when we are surrounded by pleasant colors such as blue, yellow, green, pink, and white.

We also receive color vibrations from the clothes we wear. Use the number vibrations of each color to its fullest potential. Wear a certain color to match the vibration you need at that time. If you need a large amount of vibrations from a certain number, wear a lot of that color. If you need a small vibration of a number to go along with another larger vibration, wear something small of that color. It could even be a flower.

There are color vibrations for health and for healing pain, body defects, heart problems, and universal ills such as cancer, colds, and flu. My guides tell me that colors have the same effect in our world as they do in theirs. Red is a hot color, so it is used to heal fevers. Yellow is a brilliant color and is used to heal gloomy (pessimistic) people. Blue is a cool color and is used to heal lonely people. Green is a cool color too, and it also has the brilliance of the yellow, so it is used to heal people who have cancer. Orange is a hot, brilliant color that is used to heal aches and pains. Purple is a cool, hot color and is used to heal people with blood problems.

My guides tell me that on their plane they wrap blankets of the color needed around an ailing soul and let the vibrations from the color project its healing effect through their aura. They use orange on accident victims because it removes the pain, but broken bones are healed by a healer. Cuts and bruises are wrapped in purple. They say that wearing these colors can help guard us.

I asked them about the colors of rainbows and crystals. They said that the colors in rainbows and crystals are caused by a reflection of fractured light. Raindrops fracture the light from the sun, and the bow is caused by the angle of the sun. The lower the sun sits on the horizon, the smaller the bow will be. The colors in a crystal are created in the same way. There is a fracture of the light when the sun's rays hit the angle of the crystal. The fracture causes the light to bend and it takes on color.

AGE DIGIT

The Age digit is found by adding the two ages you are during a year. Unless your birthday is January 1st or December 31st, you will be two different ages during that year. Add both ages and reduce to a single digit. This is your Age digit. For example, our George's birthday is on October 20th. In 1984 he was age 46 up to his birthday in October, then he turned 47. Adding 46 added to 47 and reducing the 93 to 12 equals 3, so in 1984 George's Age digit was 3. Use the Personal Year interpretations for the Age digit vibrations.

CASTING OUT THE 9's

When I have a group of numbers to reduce and the subtotals have no special meaning, I use a system that I call casting out the 9's. This comes in handy when you are figuring cities or states and home addresses, or anytime you are in a hurry to find a single digit. I also use it to check my figuring on all single-digit totals. It is a way of double-checking all the numbers that have been reduced to a single digit. It is the fastest way to find any single digit.

This is how it is done: In a group of numbers make a slash mark (/) through all the 9's. Then mark a / through all the numbers that total to 9 ((8+1, 7+2, 6+3, 5+4). Add up the remaining numbers and reduce to a single digit. Always mark through the number 0 in street addresses, since they add nothing. If all the numbers in the group are marked out, then your single digit would be 9, because everything in the group would have added up to and been reduced to the single digit of 9.

Example:

	C I M A R R O N,	N E W	M E X I C O
	3 9 4 1 9 9 6 5	5 5 5	4 5 6 9 3 6
First mark out 9's:	9 9 9		9
Numbers adding to 9:	3 + 6 4 + 5		4 + 5 3 + 6
Numbers not marked:	1	5 5 5	6

CIMARRON = 1, NEW = 15 = 6, MEXICO = 6,
so NEW MEXICO = 6 + 6 = 12 = 3.

Cimarron vibrates to the number 1, a place for new beginnings. New Mexico vibrates to the number 3, a pleasant or creative place.

Now it's your turn. Use a slash through the numbers only. Total and reduce.

	A U B U R N,	M A I N E
Cast out 9's:	1 3 2 3 9 5	4 1 9 5 5

Numbers adding to 9:

Numbers not marked: _____ = __   _____ = __

Did Auburn total 5? The 1, 3, 2, 3, and 9 or the 1, 3, 5, and 9 are marked out. Either way is correct. Did Maine total 6? The 4, a 5, and 9 should be marked out.

Let's do that again but use a street address this time:

(Do not use the *nd* after 182.)

	1 0 7 2 3			1 8 2 nd
Cast out the 9's:	7 2			1 8
Remember the 0:	0			
Total left is:	1	3		2

The house number equals 4, a place to work or organize. The street number totals to 2, a place to cooperate with or help others. The total vibration is 6, a beautiful home with landscaped surroundings. Using these numbers separately shows what the house is vibrating, and together, what the address is vibrating.

BASIC NUMEROLOGY CHART INTERPRETATION

When you are looking at the whole chart for interpretation, start with all the major numbers: the Path of Life, Soul Urge, Expression, Quiet Self, and Reality Number digits. Then check to see which Cycle and Attainment are in effect. These should give you a good idea of the major strengths and weaknesses of the chart. Then look at the Challenges and the minor vibrations of the rest of the chart.

When you put all the vibrations together, notice which ones are being repeated. Numbers that repeat themselves in a chart are stronger, and the vibrations they give out have a greater effect on life. Always check to see which numbers are in excess, which ones have an average amount, and which ones are lacking. If a number cannot be found in one area of the chart, check to see if it is located somewhere else and helping from there. For example, a number lacking on the Inclusion chart may be the Path of Life or one of the Cycles that are in effect during the time you are working with. This number would then be vibrating from that part of the chart and would soften the lack in the Inclusion.

If you are using the Personal cycles and the Excursion, be sure to check for numbers matching the main Paths and Cycles. These numbers could have a softening effect or they could make things a bit challenging.

Every time you work with numerology, the more familiar you will become with it. After a while all the keywords and main vibrations will come naturally to you. It's really not as hard as you may think. It just takes a little time and repetition. The more you repeat something, the more you remember it.

Keywords are the single vibrations of a number. All of the vibrations for a number can be used with that number in other places. The same number vibrates the same meaning no matter where it is located. For example, a 1 could mean a new beginning, strong leadership, or the "me first" type of explanation wherever it is located. You are the one to interpret that number in a way that conforms to your style of life or your vibrational need.

Everyone has their own set of numbers to which their life is vibrating. You are the only one responsible for how that life is lived. When you look to numbers for advice, it is your interpretation that you live by. Your interpretation of a vibration may differ from another's interpretation of that same number. This is what makes life different for everyone. No two people are really alike. Everyone has a mind of his or her own, and how you live your life is the choice that you alone must make. This is where the difference in a set of identical twins could be indicated. Unless one becomes dominant over the other their lives should be led just like the individuals they really are.

Our purpose in presenting a workbook is to help those who need help, those who want to learn on their own, or those who are being taught by a numerology teacher. We see a need for this kind of workbook, just as astrology helped many with workbooks on that subject. Numerology is sort of a condensed version of astrology, and it can be put to use for most things in a moment's notice.

Astrology and numerology complement each other if used correctly. The vibrations of the numbers foretell the same things your astrological chart does, only astrology goes deeper into interpretation of a life than this basic type of numerology does.

Our use of numbers began long ago when the ancients were given the secret meanings of the vibration of each number. They were told to use their knowledge very wisely. When they needed to know something they would use the numbers to see if the time was correct for that vibration. Just as the stars in heaven tell what time is correct for you to act, the numbers tell when the vibrations are correct for you to do what you must do to benefit from that vibration. This is what numerology is all about—using the correct vibrations to the fullest for the benefit of all humankind.

This is as far as I shall go for now. This workbook was written to help you with the basics of numerology. I hope it has simplified numerology and helped you to understand it. If you have an interest in the more advanced form of numerology, it is my hope that I have been able to help you enough so that you can progess to a better understanding of numerology as a whole.

I extend my best to you in all of your studies.

APPENDIX A

Numeric Vibrations

Keywords
(Used for All Numerology Number Meanings)

Positive	Negative
1. Individual	Self
2. Association	Subservience
3. Self-expression	Self-consciousness
4. Organized/work	Shiftlessness
5. Freedom/change	Limitation
6. Responsibility	Negligence
7. Wisdom	Misunderstanding
8. Achievement	Control/restraint
9. Compassion	Selfishness
11. Inspiration	Realism
22. Universal	Self-promotion

POSITIVE, NEGATIVE AND DESTRUCTIVE ASPECTS OF THE NUMBERS

The words listed here are to help you recognize some of the positive, negative, and destructive vibrations in hopes of helping those who may be living destructively to change to a more positive, untroubled way of life.

1

Positive

Leader, pioneer; original, independent, ambitious, active; positive, creative; intellectual, logical; courageous, forceful, progressive, determined, individual.

Negative

Selfish, lazy, egocentric, conceited, dependent, fearful; adverse, weak, stubborn, contrary, stagnating, unstable, vacillating.

Destructive

SELF-at-all-costs, iconoclastic (destroys idols and religious beliefs); dictatorial, tyrannical, antagonistic, maniacal.

2

Positive

Cooperative, considerate, adaptable, gentle; receptive, friendly, warm; partnerships, harmony, charm, diplomacy, patience, tact, association.

Negative

Subservient, shy, indifferent; careless, unconcerned, sulky; self-effacing, discontented, over-sensitive; bootlicker, spineless, unkind, doormat.

Destructive

Fraudulent, crafty, dishonest, cruel, bad-tempered, sullen; pessimistic, deceitful, cowardly.

3

Positive

Pleasant, good-natured, charming, friendly, kind, talented; optimistic, creative, imaginative, inspired, free from worry, artistic, sociable; self-expression, sense of humor.

Negative

Unpleasant, vain, boastful, extravagant; critical, gossip, trivial, shallow, careless; worrier, whiner, amateur artist, superficial, self-conscious.

Destructive

Jealous, intolerant, double-dealing, hypocritical, wasteful.

4

Positive

Organization, service, orderliness, establishment, loyalty; application, devotion, patriotism, conservatism, pragmatism; practical, dignified, patient, trusting, economical, exact.

Negative

Meddlesome, opinionated, conceited, crude, narrow, clumsy; penurious, plodding, dull, dogmatic, brusque, interfering, repressed, rigid, stern, lazy.

Destructive

Destructive, hateful, ruthless, violent, cruel; jealous, resentful, vulgar, inhumane, shiftless.

5

Positive

Freedom, change, variety; versatile, adventurous, adaptable, progressive, independent, unencumbered, unattached, sociable, understanding, curious.

Negative

Sensationalist, untrustworthy, procrastinator, inconsistent, thoughtless, irresponsible, uncultured, undependable.

Destructive

Lustful, perverse, lecherous, dissipative, overpermissive, overindulgent in drink and/or dope.

6

Positive

Home, harmony, love, marriage, domesticity, guardianship; reliable, sympathetic, understanding, stable, responsible, poised, firm, conscientious, compassionate, musically talented, idealistic, fair-minded, sacrificing, balanced, dependable, altruistic, conciliatory.

Negative

Unreasonable, stubborn, outspoken, blunt, worried, smug, meddlesome, plodding, despondent, prideful, misplaced sympathy, perfectionistic, distorted idealism, domineering.

Destructive

Tyrannical, skeptical, jealous, selfish, suspicious, cynical, egotistical.

7

Positive

Wisdom, knowledge; reserved, thoughtful, scientific, spiritual, faith, trust, stoical, skeptical, silent; thinker, deep seeker, inventor, discoverer.

Negative

Critical, aloof, rebellious, inefficient, hopeless, skeptical, confused, humiliating, nervous, misunderstands, unusual.

Destructive

Inconstant, skeptical, confused, drink, malicious, deceitful, crafty, repressed, duplicitous, concealing.

8

Positive

Accomplishment, success, self-discipline, strong character, executive ability, organization, leadership, supervision, management, practicality, thoroughness, dependability, control, self-reliance, successful, authority.

Negative

Ambition for self and wealth, schemer, poor judgment; unreliable, spineless, selfish, careless, hard, spendthrift, impatient, intolerant, anxious, unconcerned, misdirected energy, wasteful, controling, restrained.

Destructive

Miserly, bullying, tyrannical, abusive, revengeful, unjust.

9

Positive

Compassionate, impersonal, altruistic, spiritual-minded, kind, emotional, generous, idealistic, romantic, charitable, sympathetic, selfless, philanthropic, loving, tolerant, magnetic, understanding.

Negative

Nervous, frightened, fragmented, overemotional, selfish, indiscreet, unstable, impractical, unkind.

Destructive

Bitter, morose, severe, sullen, vulgar, unethical, vile, dissipative.

11

Positive

Inspirational, spiritual, idealistic, intuitive, intelligent, subjective, mystical, service to humankind, religious, artistic, inventive, poetic.

Negative

Superiority complex, dishonest, aimless, miserly, selfish, lack of understanding, fanatical, dominating, realistic, (See negative number 2).

Destructive

Dishonest, intemperate, lustful, gluttonous, degrading, crooked, mean.

22

Positive

Universal, practical, idealistic; master builder, top leader, director, manager;

achievement, honesty, government affairs, improvement, expansion.

Negative

Self-promotion, loss of ideals, anxiety, mental turmoil; begrudging service, get-rich-quick schemes, boastfulness, inferiority complex, indifference (see the negative number 4).

Destructive

Insanity, violence, black magic, crime.

GENERAL MEANINGS OF THE NUMBERS

The preceding pages listed the keywords for the numbers used in numerology. Below are some of the general meanings and vibrations for each of these numbers. You will notice that throughout this book some of the vibrations are listed under more than one number. This is because the 2 and 6 vibrations have many of the same meanings; yet they are different because the 2 may sometimes need help or a helping hand and the 6 gives it. The 4 and the 8 are work and management numbers, and unless there are a lot of 4's in someone's chart, the 8 does the work or management with stronger vibrations. The 1 and the 5 like changes and start new things. The creativity or inventive nature of the 3 could also be in the 1, in the 7, and to a lesser degree in the 5 or the 9; the 7 reflects the 3 because of the thought put into all they do, the 5 because they like to change things, and the 9 because they do what is needed to put finishing touches on their projects. The 9 is like the 2 and 6 when they are helping others.

Following this section is a listing just for Occupations.

1

The number of the individualist. One is the natural leader. It has lots of action, ambition, originality, and independence. A one's determination helps it to reach its goals. One is the number of the "me-firster." It is at the front in all actions, the first to make a move. Ones work best alone. They are the pioneers and the "mothers of inventions." They are not afraid to explore the unknown. They are very positive and creative. The 1 is a mental number; ones use their heads to solve their problems. They are not the unskilled laborers, but the professionals, the thinkers, the planners, or the creative people of our business world. If they do not own a business of their own, they are the managers, promoters, directors, or the superintendents of large firms. They prefer to lead, not follow, and will not take advice from others. They are often stubborn. They learn through experience. They are starters, not finishers. They have an outstanding character, are good companions, good-natured, talkative, and have a sense of humor. Often they are nonconformists. They attract financial rewards when their projects are for the benefit of others as well as their own. They are very sensitive regarding approval or criticism. They resent being told or shown that they are wrong. They value cleanliness, punctuality, order, and obedience, and abhor carelessness, vulgarity, and any situation that is offensive and annoying. This number needs the love and understanding within its home life to succeed to the fullest. They need a helpmate who has the same temperament and is warm and patient.

On the negative side, they can be selfish, lazy, unreasonable, and conceited. Some are shy, and others' opinions may hurt them so much that they crawl into a shell. Some may lash out with anger, surprising those around them with their terrible temper. When they get angry, they use harsh and critical words. They may be boastful, over-aggressive, or dictatorial. A few may become raving maniacs.

2

The number of the peacemaker. It cannot stand alone and must work in cooperation with others. It has the power to soothe and smooth the discord of others, for the 2 is the arbitrator, the mediator, the diplomat, or the fact finder. They are gentle, warm, patient, tactful, kind, and considerate. Cooperation is one of their main characteristics. They make good partners. Two's need love, home, peace, and harmony. They are not the kind that move around much. Some are bashful, timid, or sensitive. The 2's are collectors—some for hobbies and others as part of their jobs. They are the census takers, the pollsters, the record keepers, and statisticians. They are the healers and comforters. They like to work with detail, sometimes to the extent of overdoing it; they are fastidious. Their home and family mean much to them, but they prefer to stay in the background. Their surroundings must be comfortable, orderly, neat, clean, and beautiful. They are good hosts or hostesses. They have musical talent. Some have a natural rhythm and are good dancers. Two is the number of partnerships, associations, and marriage. They could be consultants, for they see both sides of the issue. The 2 has the desire to give peace, comfort, and beauty to all the world. A very emotional, spiritual number. Some 2's have psychic powers that should not be misused.

The negative 2's may have an inferiority complex. They dread meeting people, and are shy and timid. Some try to help others so much that they become doormats. They become easily discouraged. Negative attitudes and being uncooperative can bring about separation or divorce.

3

This is the number of self-expression. Imagination and inspiration fuel the

3's creative talents. They have a talent with words in all ways. This gift could lead them to become writers, speakers, salespersons, teachers, or entertainers who act or sing. They are artistic. Music, even composing, is found under the 3. They are cheerful, optimistic, enthusiastic, self-directed, often generous to a fault, obliging, sensitive, friendly, and good-natured. Usually they are successful. The 3's are affectionate, love deeply, and are loyal to family and home. They may be imposed upon sometime during their life by relatives or friends, putting the 3 in a self-sacrificing position. A career could be ended if criticism is taken the wrong way, since the sensitivity of the 3 makes them very self-conscious. They may avoid the person or the condition that brought about this hurt. The youthful 3's should not be reminded of their inabilities or disabilities, because this makes them ill at ease and very self-conscious. If they are not given encouragement they will live within a shell, afraid to express themselves. Their emotions need to be kept under control. Friendship, honesty, and sincerity mean a lot to the 3. They are intellectual, energetic, sociable, and natural leaders. They want beauty, joy and happiness all around them. They should follow hunches. The three has a natural attraction to money, and some 3's are interested in property and stocks and bonds. Threes also are disciplined, practical, analytical, and witty. They have the gift of prophecy. This is a mental, not a physical, number. They do well in decorative occupations. Their desire to be popular and admired leads them to many emotional experiences, including the eternal triangle. Their life makes an interesting story. Some are mediumistic. Most prefer opera to jazz. All like color and beauty.

The negative 3's are impatient, jealous, extravagant, boastful, overemotional, overtalkative, gossipy, and intolerant. They can misuse their gift with words by making cutting remarks when they become angry.

4

The hard work of this number builds the strong foundations needed to maintain all things. The 4 is practical, orderly, loyal, patient, and economical. Experience is the teacher of the 4; they learn from their own mistakes. They are courageous, honest, and have high standards. The 4's are hard workers and must always be doing something. Sometimes they become workaholics, much to the detriment of their families and their health. They are extremely ethical. They like to be consulted, not told or ordered, and they can become very stubborn. They do not like to be rushed because they want their projects to be perfect. They work and move slowly. They may miss opportunities because of their slow reactions. They need to have others around who are very active and quick thinkers. These are the people that give the 4's the incentive or the push needed to hasten their actions. The 4's are the builders of our permanent and lasting things. They build from the ground up. They are responsible, reliable, and very dependable. Once the plan is made and a project is started, they do not like changes. They are good at managing money and like to save it. They could work anywhere that money needs to be handled or managed. They work hard for their money and should not gamble. Fours are the natural mechanics and they work well with machinery. Engineering comes naturally to them. They understand technical forms and methods. The routine work is done by the 4's. They are the 9-to-5ers, the down-to-earth people. They have good business sense. The 4's need love and home in their background. In-laws can be either a help or a hindrance.

The negative 4's are lazy, clumsy, opinionated, bossy, impatient, undependable, and careless. They can be too dominant where their family and loved ones are concerned. These 4's like to have their own way in all things.

5

This is the number of variety and change. The motto of the 5 is "a rolling stone gathers no moss." This is a very active number, always on the move. Fives are inclined to try everything new. New jobs and new places interest them, and they make new friends fast. Opportunities are always coming their way. They have a restless nature and experience many ups and downs. They make quick decisions and are very impulsive. They love adventure and like to travel. They want to know what is going on in the world and would like to be part of it. Some 5's may own or run a travel bureau. Working as a tour guide also gives the 5 the change and adventure they require. Because of the curious nature of the 5, they make good detectives, investigators, insurance adjusters, writers, or reporters. The 5 is a good judge of human nature. They could be involved in the fashion world and its ever-changing seasons. The 5 is interested in spirituality, religion, or metaphysics. They are speculators and gamblers and are always looking for quick money-making ventures. Fives are always interesting and entertaining, never dull. The 5 needs to discard the old and useless to make way for new changes. They know many people and like to be among them. Many business ventures come through friends and acquaintances. The 5 is a freedom-loving number and dislikes being in a rut. Some do not marry for fear of becoming domesticated. Their mate or partner must understand the 5's active, changeable life style, and they must adjust if they want to hold them. Do not try to reform the 5. A 5 that is held back is very unhappy and restless. This is the cause of many divorces. The 5 needs to have some roots to give it stability. They have many irons in the fire and sometimes this leads to neglect and unfinished work. Routine is very boring to the 5. Their opportunities come through the public but away from the daily routine and the beaten path. The 5 may be thought of as undependable because they make light of their responsibilities. Fives should follow their hunches. There could be many changes of residences. Any line of business that has to do with transportation appeals to the 5. Their biggest success comes from doing things with and for the public.

The negative 5 is the procrastinator. Also, they can be thoughtless, inconsistent, and irresponsible. They may overindulge in drink, dope, or sex. They are very undependable. They misuse their personal freedom, which sometimes hurts others.

6

The responsibility of family, home, and the community are the concerns of the 6. They like to be the center of attention within their family and home. Their surroundings must be well-kept and beautiful. The 6 is understanding, sympathetic, reliable, dependable, and stable. They like harmony, beauty, love, and music in their home. The home atmosphere must be peaceful and orderly. Often they cannot see the faults of their loved ones. The 6 is not a manual labor number, but if they are given a job and it pays well, they will do their best to do the work required until they can find a position better suited to their ability and intelligence. The 6 prefers to work with others. They are artistic. They like the beauty of nature. Sixes are unselfish and peaceful but will fight for what they believe in. They are happiest when working for the good of humankind. They often are found working in large institutions, helping the sick and needy or teaching others. They have excellent business ability. They can be found in almost any business that has to do with the repair, remodeling, renewal, or replacement of things around homes, businesses, or institutions. Sixes apply their talents to businesses that make or market apparel or accessories; perfumes or cosmetics; jewelry or ornaments; or products that make the home comfortable and beautiful. They are generous and charitable, sometimes to a fault, and they like to receive appreciation. They learn by doing. Many use their good sense of timing in a musical career. All aspects of social work (healing or helping) appeal to them. Sixes are also good cooks. Art and cultural interests belong in their lives. They need positions with responsibility and trust. They care for the young and old alike. They live by their keen sense of right and wrong. The 6 is the helping hand when trouble knocks on the door of others. They often gain through marriage or an inheritance. Interest in boats and ships or shipping is one of the vibrations of the 6.

The negative side of the 6 can be blunt, argumentative, selfish, outspoken, and smug. They can be very domineering with their family, and they expect perfection in people. The negative 6 can be very meddlesome. They can give criticism but cannot take any themselves.

7

This is the number of wisom. The 7 is on a prolonged search for knowledge. Sevens are the silent thinkers, the seekers of the mysteries of life—always asking why, trying to discover those hidden facts. Scientific research, inventions, or new things and places to discover interest the 7. They accept nothing at face value and investigate further. This trait, along with their willingness to be silent and spend a lot of time alone, is what makes this number misunderstood or a mystery to others. Sevens like to be left alone with their books or cultural interests. Loneliness is a 7 vibration. The 7 has a studious, intellectual, analytical, and scientific mind, and they dislike manual labor. Knowledge is the path of success for the 7. They use their knowledge for the benefit of all. Their mission in life is to use their knowledge for all humankind through a special line of work. They prefer perfection over popularity. The 7 does not like suggestions from others. They have a lot of patience and should work alone. Some assistance comes unexpectedly in amazing ways. Some 7's are great artists. Whatever the 7 is working at, they consider it a learning experience and add it to their great store of knowledge. They work well with their hands, and if they apply their minds to their work they will make opportunities for themselves. The field of investigation holds much for the 7. This could be as a secret service agent, a detective, or a criminologist. They do well in medical research or in a specialized health field. The 7's often are our professors or lecturers. When the 7 is really known, they are found to be good companions. Reserved, kind, dignified, and poised. Their protective wall of silence comes down when they find that others' interest in them is real. They are like all people in that they too need love and understanding, approval, and appreciation. Attempts to make over or reform a 7 only drives them deeper inside their protective shell, possibly causing them to drink. Sevens cannot and should not be pushed, for they can become sarcastic and disagreeable. If they seem skeptical, it is only their questioning mind wanting to delve deeper. People do not understand this and take it as an insult. The 7 likes a good, well-furnished home. If their mariage is based on mutual understanding of mind and soul they should be happy and have a lasting, rewarding life. They are often miserly with their money when others are concerned, but can be lavish when it comes to their own needs. The 7 dislikes crowds and has a few close, well-chosen friends. They have an interest in spirituality, religion, or metaphysics and find mysticism a challenge. Often they find the opportunity to teach it.

The negative 7 can be very impatient. Some are crafty and some are thieves. Some can be very deceitful. Many are driven to excessive drinking because they are misunderstood. Some are very lazy.

8

The number of achievement. The love of money, material assets, and power are some of the vibrations of the 8, but these vibrations are too self-centered and can bring a loss of the same things. The 8 must learn how to balance between the spiritual and the material. When they learn that the good of humankind is the real vibration of this number and can adjust their life to that vibration, all these things come to them as a reward. The 8's are of strong character and have leadership qualities. They are practical, dependable, and have the power to succeed. The executive ability of the 8 finds them managing large business concerns, but the opportunities of the 8 come when they are doing something for the good of all. Their success comes from working to help others achieve, move ahead, or lighten their burdens. The 8 is a very active number. They do very well when they learn to manage money. They may find opportunities by investing and speculating. Eights must work for their money and not trust in luck. Eights are often bankers or working in places that handle money. The 8 prefers to lead, not follow, so they are usually managers or even owners of their own business. Big business attracts them because they do things on a large scale. They show an interest in metaphysics. The 8 has good judgment, courage, effort, sound principles, and ambition. They are good organizers, have good business sense, are proud of their family and home, and are set in their ways. Success usually brings recognition, but they should be careful when putting trust in others because it could be misplaced. Some 8's will be found in a business related to transportation. Civic and government affairs draw their interest. This could involve building on a large scale, maybe worldwide, projects that have to do with vast improvement for the benefit of all. Opportunities also come through buying, selling, trading, or even managing property. The 8's must learn how to manage money because the 8 has a tendency to make money and to lose it and then make it again, and there are many expenses with this number. Other opportunities come through sports, hotels, newspapers, magazines, publishing, healing, music, and the management of large institutions.

The negative side of the 8 is a person who demands recognition, loves power, and selfishly seeks material wealth. They are self-centered, wasteful, miserly, thoughtless, and unreliable.

9

Compassion and humanitarianism are the main vibrations of the 9. The 9 is intellectual, kind, emotional, tolerant, sympathetic, and understanding. The 9's want love, but their aim should be to give love and charity to others. The 9's compassion and love for others is given many tests. They must learn to live a selfless life. Their role is to comfort, protect, and educate humankind. The 9 has the power, kindness, sympathy, and generosity to help the old, the poor, the sick, and the needy; but they need to learn when to stop helping some, because they could be doing for other people what they should be doing for themselves. The 9 is idealistic and romantic and falls deeply in love. To crave personal power, admiration and money will destroy the 9. A 9 is divinely protected and has the power to succeed when it realizes universal love. There is usually a loss in a number 9, but they must learn to let go and make ready for the replacement that is given to advance them along their path in life. Something is always given in return for the loss in a 9. It is usually something better than what was lost, or the loss was made to make way for new opportunities for the 9 to grow and reach their goal. The 9 denotes an ending in the Cycles. This is the time to tie up the loose ends that will be carried forward into the next cycle. Some things will just come to an end in a 9. The 9 could be the time to clean house, so to speak, casting out the old, unused, or unneeded things in life, all to make way for new opportunities. If the 9 has failed and sinks to the bottom of the pit, they have the power within themselves to reach up and pull out of it and continue toward their goal. Some 9's use their creative ability as artists, entertainers, or writers to bring emotional relief to others. Many 9's use their skills in the medical field, or in any occupation where they can apply their natural perfectionism. Nines like to travel and may find that many opportunities require them to do a lot of it in order to spread their talents successfully. The 9 has a magnetic personality, one that draws people from all walks of life to them. People turn to 9's for advice, counseling, aid, comfort, or a helping hand. The 9 hates being confined to small places and small situations. Some 9's, being shy and nonaggressive, need a helping hand until they understand the power they hold within themselves. The lesson of the 9 is to leave the personal and become the impersonal—others must come first without regrets. Only then will all good things come to the 9.

The negative 9's can cause illness to themselves by letting the vibrations from resentment, jealousy and unkindness become a part of their life. The negatives show intolerance, moodiness, selfishness, and uncertainty. They are miserly and unethical. They become nervous, bitter, and frightened. Some show vulgarity and have no compassion.

11

Inspiration is the vibration of this Master Number. It is the number that possesses influence and power to move the intellect or the emotions. The 11's have an inner force that helps them bring knowledge and inspiration to humanity. Elevens are idealistic. They must leave the strictly personal behind them. Their purpose in life is to enlighten all humankind. They are intuitive and could have psychic abilities. They could be healers, physicians, or peacemakers. The 11's belong in the public eye. They could be spreading their knowledge or giving inspiration through lecturing, teaching, ministering, or spiritual advising. The 11 stands for intelligence and leadership. They make good diplomats and ambassadors who work for world peace. Elevens express themselves to others through their artistic or writing abilities. Elevens are scientists and inventors, philosophers or psychoanalysts. The 11 is the number of poetry, subjectivity, and revelation. This is a highly emotional number, and even though they look cool and calm they could be high-strung and nervous. The vibrations of the number 2 also apply to the number 11, except that the 11 is on a higher plane and more is expected of this Master Number.

The negative consider themselves above all else. They could be aimless, dishonest, irritable, indifferent, selfish, or unkind. They thrust their will upon others. Some become thieves and crooks.

22

Universal love is the vibration of this Master Number. The 22 is the master builder. Everything they do is on a large scale. Their role is to serve or build for the benefit of all humankind. The 22's are not followers—they are the leaders, the managers, or the directors. They are honest, practical, intuitive, and have their feet planted firmly on the ground. They have the ability to see plans on a large scale. They beautify while they build. Their interests lie with large corporate or international concerns. The 22's are also interested in world peace. They work before or for the public, and everything they do contributes to the general welfare of all humankind. The 22's open new fields and blaze new trails. They should follow their hunches. They must keep their nerves under control. They go to extremes and should guard against becoming excessive. The 22's are very logical people. They make good reformers and promoters. They could be efficiency experts because they know how to schedule, organize, and manage. They are national or international diplomats or ambassadors. A 22 could become the president of a large firm or the leader of a country. They have the ability to improve and expand, but they must be selfless. The vibrations of the number 4 also apply to the number 22, except that the 22 is on a higher plane and is more in the professional world than in the manual labor world.

The negative 22's look for the get-rich-quick schemes. Some could be boastful, indifferent, or rebellious. Some have an inferiority complex. Some engage in crime. This negative number could indicate a tendency toward a mental disorder or possible insanity.

OCCUPATIONS

Each number derived from the birth date and each letter and its numeric value in the full name give indications of talents and possible occupations or careers. Listed below are a few occupations, places of work, and vibrations for each number that should be considered when choosing employment. They are not meant in any way to represent all the vibrations that each number holds, so when you see single words such as nature, furniture, institutions, hotels, etc., precede them with the words "anything having to do with." Some vocations are listed with more than one number. Take the farmer for example; this occupation would fit the vibrations of the number 4 because of the hard work, management, and organization involved. It would also have the vibration of a number 6 because farmers grow and supply the food for homes, hotels, restaurants, hospitals, etc.

Look also at the complete numerology chart to see if there are numbers repeating themselves in the major places. These could be clues to your greatest talent or best career. The Path of Life digit shows if there is natual talent. The Expression tells where to look for opportunities. The Soul Urge indicates what the self really wants to do. The Reality Number shows what to work toward. The Inclusion chart tells how you will apply yourself with what you have.The Planes of Expression chart shows how you would carry out a job. The Life Cycles and Attainments indicate where you are at present and what you should accomplish. The Life Challenges show which barriers stand in the way of accomplishing these things. Analyze all of these when selecting the best job for you.

1

Leader, manager, overseer, inventor, engineer, executive, explorer, designer, department head, writer, lawyer, promoter, illustrator, artist, antique dealer, dressmaker, mining, business owner, lecturer, teacher, professor, medicine, surgery, health matters, governmental activities, bookstores, composer, musician, libraries, art galleries, museums, teacher of religion, originator of fashion, amusement, entertainment, or any unique idea.

2

Arbitrator, diplomat, ambassador, politician, psychologist, student, teacher, secretary, statistician, companion, homemaker, dancer, musician, artist, psychic, religion, banking, science, adviser, radio, T.V., messenger, electricity, telephone, technical, mechanical, medicine, consultant, vocalist, orator, spiritual healer, accountant, finances, organization worker, administration, treasurer, teller, paymaster, fact finder, electronics, control of money, brain surgeon, laboratory technician, nerve specialist, orchestra leader, appraiser, bookkeeper, host or hostess, collector (even as a hobby), travel, liquid, fine machinery, delicate instruments, literature, or peacemaker.

3

Writer, actor, singer, lecturer, interior decorator, designer, commercial art, composing, fine artist, entertainer, critic, society organizer, welfare worker, clergy, missionary, jeweler, milliner, dressmaker, stock market, real estate, mechanical arts, soldier, boxer, medium, businessperson, student, chef, gift shops, author, crafts, musician, theater, illustration, toys, bonds, commentator, sales, advertising, education, investments, travel, fashions, amusements, cosmetics, beauty parlors, bakeries, restaurants, libraries, kindergarten, rest homes, aviation navy, army, candy, food, printing, publishing, or self-expression.

4

Builder, contractor, organizer, commercial art, real estate, buying, selling, education, public utilities, employment agencies, administration, management, engineering, mason, electrician, plumber, skilled craftsperson, technician, economist, statistician, professor, instructor, executive, accountant, scientist, physician, surgeon, chemist, horticulturist, farmer, musician, shopkeeper, repairperson, ministry, soliciting, hiring, regulator, campaign promotor, documents, legal papers, lender, legal activities, commodities, supplier of daily needs, mechanic, manufacturing, fabric maker, furniture maker, cabinetmaker, research, investigation, law and order, geologist, biologist, archaeologist, explorer, research chemist, nature, rancher, dairies, landscaper, money management, military, head of any undertaking, stores, shops, offices, 9-to-5er.

5

Public interest, salesperson, advertising, stocks and bonds, travel agent, detective, secret service, investigator, courier, truck driver, legal undertakings, actor, promoter, inventor, civic leader, senator, lawyer, editor, platform speaker, drama critic, publicity, public entertainment, reporter, writer, government official, politician, metaphysics, sports, games, amusements, carnivals, circus, campgrounds, parks, entertainer, commercial art, clothing stylist, speculator (not gambling), conselor, researcher, scientific study, analysis, interpreter, languages, changing events, traveler, airlines, railroads, bus lines, trucking, shipping, sightseeing guide, clown, speaker, lecturer, clothing stores, administrator, company head, organizer, judge, religious presentation, teacher, psychologist.

6

Artist, cook, chef, gardener, interior decorator, singer, actor, teacher, doctor, nurse, poet, engineer, rancher, farmer, lawyer, landscaper, miner, horticulturist, potter, commercial artist, painter, furniture line, hotels, institutions, hospitals, restaurants, apartments, welfare work, boats, ships, shipping, healer, arbitrator, speaker, radio, religious work, theater, home builder, dealer in food, literature, dealer in home necessities, playwright, opera, illustrator, painter, decorator, philosopher, historian, theorist, professor, scientist children's books, health healing, manufacturing and marketing commodities, clothing, cosmetics, accessories, perfume, health stores, rest homes, geologist, zoologist, bacteriologist, irrigation, art, beauty, cultural interest, child care, animals, flowers, story-teller, livestock, all lines of reform or education.

7

Professor, teacher, technical writer, scientist, inventor, explorer, psychic, metaphysics, educator, lawmaker, banker, broker, accountant, weaver, watchmaker, editor, naturalist, astronomer, theologian, priest, minister, historian, chemist, technician, lawyer, surgeon, statistician, insurance agent, laboratory worker, detective, secret service agent, criminologist, artist, musician, calculation, analysis, mathematical pursuits, chemistry, lab work, dietetics, research, criminal investigation, all business requiring skill, law, engineering, movies, radio, T.V., carving, etching, delicate art objects, organist, bookkeeping, recorder, specialist, charts, graphs, maps, medicine, medical research, brain specialist, books, literature, gourmet chef, clubs, inns, teacher of metaphysics, lecturer.

8

Director, manager, supervisor, writer, literature, education, finance, shipping, consulting, transportation, organizer of charities, executive, business owner, coaching, sports, explorer, broker, bondsman, commercial magnate, manufacturer, corporation head, promoter, newspaper executive, property and estate manager, instructor, superintendent, government position, civil engineer, insurance agent, real estate agent, architect, professional arts and sciences, statistics, hotels, summer resorts, overseer, publishing, mountain climber, nurse, work with animals, mystic, metaphysics, industry, commerce, large organizations, controller, efficiency expert, political management, research, fact gatherer, loans, trusts, magazine publisher, correspondent, reporter, intelligence service, judge, counselor, physician, hospital administrator, antiques, museums, art galleries, editing, archaeology, drama, music, organist, character analyst, caretaker at mental hospitals and institutions.

9

Civic or public service, welfare worker, charity, hospitals, institutions, non-profit service, clubs, artist, teacher, writer, dramatic actor, surgeon, doctor, nurse, lawyer, philanthropist, preacher, reformer, orator, painter, musician, composer, adviser, counselor, judge, importer, designer, architect, cabinetmaker, upholsterer, literature, movies, foods, health matters, travel, governmental activities, personnel office, beautify surroundings, mechanical arts, designer, religious activites, large groups of people, foreign contacts, foreign businesses, humanitarian, publishing, mimic, comedian, technician repairing works of art, people's comfort, inventor, useful industry, luxuries for people.

11

Artist, teacher, scientist, inventor, explorer, reformer, healer, critic, peacemaker, philosopher, psychologist, lecturer, minister, evangelist, religious writer, diplomat, ambassador, spiritual adviser, psychic, seer, charity worker, welfare worker, leader, psychoanalyst, inspired actor, electronics technician, aviation, spiritualism, being in the limelight, inspires others.

22

Builder on a large scale, organizer of public affairs, leadership, manager, director, professor, teacher, diplomat, public benefactor, writer, international concerns, large cooperatives, director of world affairs, general welfare of public, engineer, architect, bridge builder, dam builder, high-rise buildings, expansive undertakings, worldwide shipping, buyer for large concerns, rulers, head of large institutions, reformer, efficiency expert, ambassador, national and international recognition, president, governor, benefit the world.

APPENDIX B

Alphabet Values and Meanings

Alphabet Values and Meanings

These are some of the key vibrations of the English alphabet. The first bold-faced word at the beginning of each letter's meaning indicates its classification on the Planes of Expression chart: Mental, Physical, Emotional, or Intuitive.

Numeric Values of the English Alphabet

1	2	3	4	5	6	7	8	9
A	B	C	D	E	F	G	H	I
J	(K)	L	M	N	O	P	Q	R
S	T	U	(V)	W	X	Y	Z	

The letter *K* equals the Master Number 11.
The letter *V* equals the Master Number 22.

A

Mental The vibrations of the *A* come from the 1. This letter is the first in the alphabet, so it will always indicate being first in all things. The *A* is very determined and headstrong and will not take orders from anyone. It must lead and will not follow without trying to direct. The *A* stands for independence. *A*'s are original, innovative, and creative leaders. They must learn through direct experience; they are beginners, not finishers; and they seek change and adventure. Their ambition, aspiration, and self-direction will guide them straight to their goal. Some are very agressive. The *A*'s are the creators, the trailblazers.

B

Emotional   Sentimental, friendly, needs intimacy; subjective, shy, jealous, psychic. Has deep, emotional love affairs. Follower not a leader; needs affection and mothering. Self-contained, resourceful, inventive. Likes to stay in one place. Intuitive, dreamer, mediator, diplomat. Extremely sensitive, often timid; lacks self-assertiveness. Seeks encouragement and appreciation. Needs to develop a strong will. Loves home, needs companionship, cannot work alone. Usually has pleasing personality. Gentle, quiet—lovable disposition and fine temperament. *B* in the beginning of a name represents organization. *B* stands for cooperation, tact, and diplomacy. Since this letter has the duality of the 2, a person with the *B* can be sometimes positive and sometimes negative. Their weakest trait is under-valuing themselves.

C

Intuitive   Self-expressive, enterprising, articulate, impressive, eloquent, inventive, communicative, strong, energetic, social, creative, and imaginative. The *C* has all the vibrations of the 3, expressing its pleasant attitude, many talents, and creativity. They do their best to make others happy. When put to good use, *C*'s talents could involve music, art, dancing, acting, or singing. Some are unaware of their psychic abilities. Most *C*'s have many irons in the fire, scattering their energies in too many places. Some are indecisive, often exaggerate, and have difficulty in managing money.

D

Physical   Realistic, businesslike, down-to-earth, and practical. A hard worker, assistant, laborer, servant, aide, advocate. *D* is a sign of travel if business or work is involved. Straightforward, efficient, capable, pragmatic, sensible, just; intellectual, keen mind, sometimes overcritical, has a tendency to oppose everything (stands in own light). The 4 vibration makes the *D* a manager, organizer, supervisor, boss, or builder and sometimes causes them to become a slave to their job or business. They crave appreciation and recognition, are honest, true, constant, thrifty, and have a good judge of value. World businesses would be lost without the organization, management, and concern of the *D*. They need to control their temper, for it could affect their health and ruin business opportunities. They have order and intensity of purpose and belong in the business world of mining, manufacturing, or real estate, etc.

E

Physical This letter denotes many things and many changes. Freedom and variety are its top vibrations. The *E* must seek change to be happy. They are practical, have foresight and a versatile mind, are energetic, enthusiastic, good talkers, and adaptable. The desire for travel and the urge for new adventures keep them moving. They make good salespeople. They like the challenge of exploring deeply into the mysteries of life. Their imaginations spur them on. It is hard for them to stay in one place for too long. Many *E*'s in a name could cause one to be too impulsive or fickle. The vibrations of the *E* (5) are associated with physical love affairs or marriage.

F

Intuitive Dependable, accountable, respected, hard worker, responsible, constructive, cheerful, cooperative, home-oriented, ethical, burden-bearer. They are reliable, honest, conscientious, trustworthy. The *F* must live the life of one who does for others. They have a deep love of home but often are a slave to it. They love a beautiful home and surroundings. Marriage and children fill a need in their lives. They are the people who make parks, playgrounds, city gardens, or other areas the beautiful places the rest of us enjoy. They love nature and the quiet and peace that goes with it. *F*'s have firm opinions, do not like criticism, and cannot take advice. Not easily convinced.

G

Mental Analytical, knowledgeable, perceptive, astute; researcher, scholar, thinker, well-read, informed, introspective, aloof; needs comprehension to keep from encountering misfortune. Outgoing, secret, determined, very original in thought and action, inclined toward intellectual and philosophical pursuits; has strong willpower, often psychic, imaginative. Lack self-expression—often misunderstood by others because of their silent nature. They have the patience to develop a vast store of wisdom. The vibration of the 7 gives this letter the mental capabilities needed to become doctors, lawyers, teachers, professors, or any occupation in which brain is used more than brawn. Sevens are quiet, studious, read many books, and have the ability to retain what they read. They possess vivid imaginations and have the determination to overcome obstacles.

H

Mental Manager, director, agent, designer; moves from the tangible to the intangible but with wavering conclusions. Their executive abilities make them capable of great achievement in business and finance. They are fluent talkers, good mixers, and very active. Their analytical mind depends more on reason than on intuition. Often they seek proof when it comes to spiritual matters. *H*'s like to travel, which may have a connection with their line of work. Here the number 8 is vibrating, meaning that the letter *H* needs proper management in all things. Money is the root of most of their problems, and mismanagement could cause many ups and downs in life. *H* people are hard workers and accomplish great tasks by staying with their projects until they are completely finished. They have the ability to work with small details and be precise. Their life needs management and order for success.

I

Emotional *I*'s are creative, imaginative, intuitive, and sympathetic; sometimes oversensitive or high-strung, vacillating, nervous, tense. They make good inspirational speakers, lecturers, actors, and musicians. They are intellectual, analytical, and critical. Often they will notice shortcomings before goodness. *I*'s need periods of meditation. Sometimes they are too serious and are inclined to see the pathetic side of life. When the vibration of the number 9 is in effect, it gives the letter *I* humanitarian impulses. These vibrations make our ambassadors, diplomats, social workers, missionaries, or those who give selfless service to others. When the 9 vibrates, it says now is the time to work for humankind. The *I* must give to be happy, yet some give too much because they do not have the ability to say no. That's when the letter *I* becomes nervous and high-strung—their emotions say they should help, yet they know they are spending time that is needed elsewhere.

J

Mental Leadership, determination, initiative, inventiveness, imaginative, original, idealistic, works for improvement. The *J* vibrates like the letter *A*, except stronger. When a *J* is in a name it says "Here I am. I will be the one to do what needs to be done." When the 1 vibrates as strong as it does in the *J*, it is very headstrong; the mental abilities take over. These are the people who make the scientific discoveries, the inventions, the improvements. Many are writers. They are the doers, the ones making the changes life needs to progress. Highly motivated by surroundings. Money-making is important to them; they are unhappy without it. *J*'s are systematic, orderly, good-natured, and have a happy disposition. They may get hurt because of attachments; when friendship is broken, their faith also ends.

K

Intuitive A Master Number letter with a high spiritual vibration. *K*'s are receptive to life. They follow their hunches, sometimes receiving inspiration from divine revelation. They are dreamers, often difficult to understand, and they have strong likes and dislikes but are tolerant. *K*'s are sophisticated and appreciate the beautiful and the artistic. They follow the straight and narrow to success. These Old Soul people have the knowledge of the ancients stored in their subconscious minds just waiting to help others, which is their mission in life. When the *K* vibrates to the 11, it has all of the above indications. When it vibrates to the single digit of the 2, it must work in cooperation with others. While the 2 needs a helping hand, the 11 extends it. Where the 2 works in partnership with others and needs others to aid them,the 11 gives that aid. (The 2 vibrations are listed in Appendix A and should be taken into account if the strong vibrations of the 11 are too much for someone to live up to.) All letter *K*'s want or have few friends. All should work to develop their spiritual nature.

L

Mental Talented, creative, inventive, imaginative, skillful; clever, versatile, intelligent, gifted, and bright. *L*'s love life, are very sociable, and have great reasoning powers. They are energetic, full of push, and always searching for new things. The *L* vibrates toward the pleasant things in life. They like their artistic talents to be noted. They love music, art, and picturesque places, and enjoy them as often as possible. They love to travel. Their love of entertainment makes for a fun-filled life. *L*'s favor justice for all and make good managers and organizers; they are happiest when feeling useful. They desire public approval and usually have good manners and a good speaking or singing voice.

M

Physical Intellectual, thorough, practical, hard worker, is capable of leading. The *M* is bound to materiality and form. They are realistic, efficient, hard-headed, sensible, pragmatic, businesslike, and shrewd. Some are natural homemakers; others are mechanically minded. They adapt to most situations. Some are workaholics, but some are lazy and undisciplined. This is the letter of the builder, the foundation maker, the dream-come-true person. The practical *M* manages investments such as properties, stock, bonds, bank accounts, or businesses wisely. The homemaker *M* manages the home, the budget, or personal investments pertaining to family matters.

N

Mental Many changes: jobs, homes, transportation modes, friends, or mental persuasions for the vibrations of the *N* embody variety, improvement, modernization, modification, and new activities. *N* is adaptable, versatile, confident, clever, resourceful, and adjusts easily. Its changes could bring love and marriage.

A vivid imagination nurtures fantasies, inventions, creativity, or other inspirations. They have a need to stabilize their lives, because insecurity and instability do not make for happy homes, good jobs, or financial gains. *N*'s have a brilliant mind, yet they may vacillate when making decisions. Sometimes they are nervous and restless. Because of their many experiences, conversation is varied and interesting and usually not boring.

O

Emotional *O*'s are a circle incased around themselves—self-enclosed or close-minded; stubborn and unyielding. They look out for themselves. They are quiet, inconspicuous, frugal, conservative, protective, poised, and secure. They are responsible, strong inspirational, yet willful and brooding. *O*'s have a pleasing personality and have many friends, with whom they are faithful and true. Uses own judgment. The love of home vibration of the 6 could indicate many changes or moves while always looking for something better. *O*'s need home, love, and marriage in their lives. Because they hold things inside, they tend to suffer in silence.

P

Mental *P*'s are self-sufficient; they lack will power, yet they love to study. The *P* is semi-enclosed, so it has the ability to know others are needed to advance. They are interested in metaphysics and would make good teachers along those lines. Most have talent and an inner urge to travel to gain knowledge. They are silent, yet talk for long periods if a topic is known and liked; knowledge is a strong point. *P*'s are endowed with inner intuition, which is their best teacher. They are very strong minded where their life is concerned. This 7 vibration is stronger because it is on a higher octave. The 7's knowledge for the *P* means learning from experience. They may travel to the end of the Earth to obtain knowledge on one subject.

Q

Intuitive *O* is not a true letter, yet as it is used in the English alphabet it vibrates to the 8. The *Q* has enclosed feelings with a way out—the *Q* has alternatives. Most are business minded and feel strong responsibility toward all it holds. All *Q*'s are quiet and comtemplative, yet they will talk about what interests them. They have a very friendly attitude and are good at parties. Many have strong material instincts and would make good managers because they like business challenges. All like recognition. While the *Q* is personable, they sometimes can be quiet and hard to know. They hold their problems within until they realize a solution or get help.

R

Emotional Robust, strong-willed, cooperative. The positive type *R* gives help, but the negative type expects it. Those who lead a positive life have a kindheartedness not found in others. Some are very concerned about others—they don't ask, they just act. The *R* has the ability to become famous. *R* has the inner sense to know right from wrong. Most of them are honest, kind, true, and have no qualms about being called upon when needed. *R*'s are the peacemakers, the humanitarians. Many *R*'s in a name show a very compassionate person.

S

Emotional Strong-willed, adaptable, yet wavers if unsure. This letter has many meanings—it could be the most misunderstood letter in the alphabet. Some *S*'s are headstrong, while others wait for an opening to take place before they act. Some *S*'s have leadership qualities, while others need to be led or shown how to begin; then they take hold. They may waver like the shape of the letter *S*. Many *S*'s in a name adds to stability. Those *S*'s who know what they want in life are very determined to reach that goal. The *S* vibrates to the number 1 in so far as they are original, independent, and self-oriented. One side of the *S* that does not always vibrate to the world is the emotional side. *S*'s do not want others to know that they have strong emotional feelings. They need to show the strong, forceful side, yet they represent one of the most emotional letters in the alphabet. They have a need to express themselves with strength, love, sorrow, or even rage.

T

Emotional This, too, is an emotional letter. Having a strong 2 vibration, most *T*'s make good partners, companions, and friends, and they depend upon others to guide them. They follow the vibrations of the 2 stronger when others help or cooperate in all that they do. When *T*'s learn that they, too, are needed, they live a happier life. Two gives the *T* a certain amount of dependence upon others. When the 2 vibrates here it tells the *T* it must learn to give and take the helping hand, *T*'s have nervous tensions and are sometimes prone to self-pity. When they are helped or being helpful, their emotional state becomes calm and gentle. Some *T*'s are pillars of strength. When a letter stronger than the *T* surrounds it in a name, it strengthens the *T*. When the first letter is the *T*, it says "I am needing the strength of a helping hand." Help could come through the strenth of an *A* following it or through other parts of the name: first, middle, or last. The *T* depends upon others if alone, and will give help to others if it has strong adjacent vibrations—a double *T* for example.

U

Intuitive The *U* enjoys life, friends, groups, pleasant surroundings, and good books. They are artistic and creative in one way or another. Their talents are reflected in the 3 vibation. The *U* needs to be known and must have positive friends who show a variety of talents. The *U* has to exhibit, publish, or perform at least once in their lifetime. They need to express themselves. They have strong wills, are steadfast and reliable, mostly honest, trustworthy, and true. *U*'s have all the qualities of the 3 in higher octaves.

V

Intuitive A Master Number letter. The *V* will always vibrate to working with large projects. when the vibrations lean toward the Master Number 22, those projects will be for worldwide or universal use. When leaning toward the 4 vibration, the work habits will be stronger to the extent of becoming a workaholic. The *V* will always be doing something constructive, will always be busy. They do things with precision, down to the smallest detail, and will not give final approval to their project unless it is flawless. Most *V*'s are clean, neat, orderly, well groomed, fastidious, and conscientious.

W

Physical This letter has the strong vibration of the 5, which is a change number. Fives move about from hither to yon, changing jobs often, yet they like change because it usually adds to their vast knowledge. The *W* really has a twofold purpose: it cries for change yet teaches responsibility. The vibrations of the 5 are harder on this letter than most other 5's, because the *W* must be responsible to those who make their changes possible. They are well versed in most subjects, so they make good speakers, good friends, and are called upon to liven up parties. They can become boring if one topic is talked about too long. Those with a *W* in their name like travel and will go at the drop of the hat. They do best in some line of work where travel or adventure is involved. They make good travel agents. They have a strong love of nature. *W*'s like their freedom and independence, and they seek variety and new activities. They are always looking for ways to improve their mind, their job, or things around them. They are proud-spirited, versatile, quick learners, and prosperous in business. They need love and understanding.

X

Emotional The strong vibration of the 6 makes this letter one of the most helpful letters in the alphabet. *X*'s have many talents and are always putting them to good use in one way or another. They are happiest when doing something in or around the home. They love to rearrange their furniture. They have many friends, and their home is always open to all. They need to associate with others and prefer the company of talented or knowledgeable people. These are the peacemakers, the stabilizers in life. They must be married and have a home and children to be happy. They are very considerate, fashionable, and like peace and quiet. Their emotional, caring nature and their talents carry them through life.

Y

Intuitive This letter, like the 7, is misunderstood. *Y*'s like solitude, which gives them time to study, think, and meditate. They are the hermits in life. They are very intelligent and have a strong interest in most things. They would like to know everything. The stronger vibration of the 7 makes the *Y* delve into the depths of the hidden, the unknown, the mysteries in life. They may do a lot of traveling or reading in search of answers. The *Y*'s make good teachers, professors, scientists, doctors, religious leaders, or metaphysicians. They are studious, giving a lot of thought to anything interesting to them. They are silent, thoughtful, skeptical, and reserved, yet faithful, trustworthy, and refined.

We must add a note to this letter. In some cases it may sound like another letter, the *E* or the *I* for instance, so we suggest that in cases like this you look to those letters to see if the correct vibration you feel is there. Let's use the name "Yvonne" for an example. Some pronounce it "Evonne"(*E*von), in which case the *E* is strongest, so look through *E*'s meaning for vibrations that may match that person better.

Z

Emotional The high octave of the 8 makes this letter very business-minded. The *Z*'s have an inner sense that vibrates toward large business dealings or financial matters. When the *Z* works with money it knows what must be done to be successful. Most *Z*'s are honest, faithful, reliable, and hard workers. They can manage, lead, organize, promote, advise, and direct. They have high hopes, big dreams, and are big spenders. Willing to promote, they spend money to make money. When money is involved, they must use care because the vibrations of the 8 also cause losses if mismanaged or wrong investments are made. *Z*'s are well liked. They are business executives, CEOs, managers, stockbrokers, bankers, and advisers. The *Z* is self-confident, disciplined, intelligent, understanding, intellectually capable, intuitive, and organized. These people are very emotional yet controlled, but they may lose their tempers if pushed. When they are given an assignment, their energy level rises dramatically. If they are stalemated or between jobs, their energy level becomes very low; therefore the *Z* must remain busy to be happy. They must guard against excess in all things, since good management is their main vibration. Some may become workaholics.

APPENDIX C

Blank Numerology Forms

These blanks can be used as additional worksheets while using this workbook, as extras, or as test papers for students. Refer to corresponding sections in the text for more detailed explanations on how to fill each out.

Use single digits only.

Birth Date: _____   Name: _____

    Month   _____   Formative Cycle   _____

    Day   _____   Productive Cycle _____

    Year   _____   Harvest Cycle   _____

                 _____Path of Life

                            Birth Day Vibrations _____

Birth Digit   _____   Day Challenges _____

                                Day Gift _____

Life's Challenges: _____ Major _____ 1st Minor _____ 2nd Minor _____ Added

Year	(Age)	Path of Life	Life Cycles	Attainments or Pinnacles	Life's Challenges	Name Vibs.	Name Challenge
	Birth (3) (6) (9)				Major	Expr	Exp Chal
	(18)					S.U.	SU Chal
	(27)				First Minor	Q.S.	QS Chal
	(36)					First Vowel	
	(45)				Second Minor		
	(54)					Reality Number	
	(63)				Added Minor		
	(72)						
	(81)						
	(90)						

	FIRST NAME	MIDDLE NAME	LAST NAME	
SU digits	___	___	___	= SU ___
Sub totals:	___	___	___	
Value of Vowels:	_____	_____	_____	
FULL NAME:	_____	_____	_____	
Numeric Values:	___	___	___	
Expression Sub totals:	___	___	___	
Expression digits:	___	___	___	= EXP ___
Consonant Values:	_____	_____	_____	
Quiet Self Sub totals:	___	___	___	
QS digits:	___	___	___	= QS ___

SOUL URGE CHALLENGE____QUIET SELF CHALLENGE____EXPRESSION CHALLENGE____

INCLUSION

RULING PASSION	_____
RULING PASSION CHALLENGES	_____
SUBCONSCIOUS SELF	_____
CORNERSTONE	_____
KEY NUMBER	_____
ECCENTRICITY	_____
KEY LETTER	_____
BALANCE NUMBER	_____
FIRST VOWEL	_____
ACHIEVEMENT	_____
CAPSTONE	_____
KEYSTONE	_____
NAME CHARACTERISTIC	_____

PLANES OF EXPRESSION

	Mental	Physical	Emotional	Intuitive	Totals
Inspired Creative					
Dual Vacillating					
Balanced Grounded					
Totals					

PATH OF LIFE

Write the birth date you are using here: _____

Month of Birth _____ (1–12)

Day of Birth _____ (1–31)

Year of Birth _____ (four digits)

Total _____

Reduce _____ = __ + __ + __ + __ = _____ = __ + __ = __ P. of L.

LIFE CYCLES

FORMATIVE CYCLE = Month of Birth ____ = __ + __ = ____.

PRODUCTIVE CYCLE = Day of Birth ____ = __ + __ = ____.

HARVEST CYCLE = Year of Birth ____ = 1 + 9 + __ + __ = __ = __ + __ = ____.

Do the following to find the Life Cycle durations:

A UNIVERSAL YEAR DIGIT is found by reducing the year number to a single digit. (Example 1 + 9 + 8 + 3 = 21 = 2 + 1 = 3 U.Y.)

Place the year number you will be using here_____and reduce_____.

Birth digit: Find your Birth digit by filling in the blanks below.

        Birth Month   (1-12)

        Birth Day   +_____ (1-31)

        Total and reduce   = __ + __ = _____ = BIRTH DIGIT (B.D.)

To find the year the Formative Cycle ends and the Productive Cycle begins, fill in the blanks below with your numbers.

        Year of Birth   (use all four numbers)

        Add age 27   + _27_

        Reduce

                = __ + __ + __ + __ = ____ = __ + __ = __ U.Y.

Add this to the Birth digit to find the Personal Year.

        U.Y.

        B.D.   +___

        Add, Reduce.   = ____ + ____ = _____ P.Y.

Use this space below to add or subtract the years needed if not a 1 Personal Year.

Fill in the blanks below with your numbers to find the date when the Productive Cycle ends and Harvest Cycle begins.

    Year of birth

    Add age 57   + $\underline{\ 57\ }$

    Reduce   = __ + __ + __ + __ = ____ U.Y.

This number (U.Y.) is added to your Birth Digit(B.D.).

    U.Y.

    B.D.   +____

    Reduce   = ____ + ____ = _____ P.Y.

If not a 1 P.Y., ADD or SUBTRACT the number of years needed in the space below. This same number of years also needs to be added or subtracted to correct the age.

BIRTH DAY VIBRATIONS

Day of Birth   ____ = __ + __ = __ Birth Day Vibrations

Challenges of Birth Day (1–9 are own digit challenges. 11–31 subtract below.)

Day of Birth   ____ = __ − __ = Birth Day Challenge.

Birth Day Gift (used to aid the challenge of the Birth Day)

The Ultimate Number   9

Subtract Birth Day Challenge   −__

Equals the Birthday Gift: __

ATTAINMENTS (PINNACLES)

You will see just how easy it is to find the Attainment durations and their digits when you fill in the blanks below with your numbers.

		(example)
(Always use number 36 here)	36	36
Subtract Path of Life	−	− 7
1st Attainment ends at age and second begins		29
Add 9 more years	+ 9	+ 9
2nd Attainment ends at age and Third begins		38
Add 9 more years	+ 9	+ 9
3rd Attainment ends at age and Fourth begins		47

The Fourth Attainment runs for the rest of life.

FINDING THE ATTAINMENT DIGITS

FIRST ATTAINMENT: (month of birth digit plus day of birth digit)

Month of Birth Digit

Add Day of Birth Digit   +____

Reduce   = __ + __ = ____ 1st Attainment

SECOND ATTAINMENT: (day of birth digit plus year of birth digit)

Day of Birth Digit

Add Year of Birth Digit   +____

Reduce   = __ + __ = ____ 2nd Attainment

THIRD ATTAINMENT: (The total of the First and Second Attainments)

Digit of First Attainment

Add Digit of 2nd Attainment +____

Reduce to single digit   = __ + __ = ____ 3rd Attainment

FOURTH ATTAINMENT: (The birth month plus the of birth year digit)

Month of Birth Digit

Add Year of Birth Digit +____

Reduce if needed   = __ + __ = ____ 4th Attainment

LIFE'S CHALLENGES (Attainment Challenges)

You always subtract the smaller digit from the larger digit when you are working with Challenges, regardless of where it is placed.

Birth Month Digit

Subtract Birth Day Digit   −____

                                            = 1st Minor Challenge

Birth Day Digit

Subtract Birth Year Digit   −____

                                            = 2nd Minor Challenge

1st Minor Challenge Digit

Subtract 2nd Minor Digit   −____

                                            = Major Challenge

ADDITIONAL CHALLENGE (used only if this number differs from the other three challenges)

Birth Month Digit

Subtract Birth Year Digit   −____

                                            = Additional Minor Challenge

UNIVERSAL YEAR AND PERSONAL YEAR

YEAR you are using _____.

UNIVERSAL YEAR: $1 + 9 + \_\_ + \_\_ = \_\_ = \_\_ + \_\_ = \_\_$ U.Y.

PERSONAL YEAR

Birth Digit	(month plus day of birth)
Plus U.Y. Digit	+____ (from above)
Reduce	$= \_\_ + \_\_ = \_\_$ P.Y.

A quick way to figure a Personal Year is to add the Path of Life digit to the age you *will be* in the year that you are working with.

Path of Life Digit

Plus the age in year you are using   +____

Reduce $= \_\_ + \_\_ = \_\_$ P.Y.

PERSONAL YEAR PINNACLES

(1)

U.Y.

Add B.D.   +___

Reduce   = __ + __ = __ January 1st to March 31st.
                                (Pinnacle duration)

(2)

B.D.

Add P.Y.   +___

Reduce   = __ + __ = __ April 1st to June 30th.

(3)

Digit (1) above

Add digit (2) above   +___

Reduce   = __ + __ = __ July 1st to September 30th.

(4)

U.Y.

Add P.Y.   +___

Reduce   = __ + __ = __ October 1st to December 31st.

PERSONAL YEAR CHALLENGES

(subtract smaller digit from larger digit)

U.Y.

Subtract B.D.   −___

Reduce   = 1st MINOR CHALLENGE

P.Y.

Subtract B.D.   −___

Reduce   = 2nd MINOR CHALLENGE

Digit (1)

Subtract digit (2)   −___

Reduce   = MAJOR CHALLENGE

Additional Challenge only if the digit found is different from those above.

U.Y.

Subtract P.Y.   −___

Reduce   = ADDITIONAL MINOR CHALLENGE

Personal Month: Month you are using _____ . Its digit _____.
A personal month is found by adding the P.Y. digit to the Month Digit.

P.Y. ____

Plus Month digit +____

Total = ____ + ____ = ____ P.M. (PERSONAL MONTH)

PERSONAL MONTH PINNACLES

Digit of month you are using _____.

(1)   Duration:

P.Y.

Add Month +___

Reduce = __ + __ = 1st through 7th of the month.

(2)

P.Y.

Add P.M. +___

Reduce = __ + __ = 8th through 14th of the month.

(3)

Digit (1)

Add digit (2) +___

Reduce = __ + __ = 15th through 21st of the month.

(4)

Month

Add P.M. +___

Reduce = __ + __ = 22nd thru remainder of month.

PERSONAL MONTH CHALLENGES

(subtract smaller digit from larger digit)

P.Y.

Subtract Month   −__

                        = FIRST MINOR CHALLENGE

P.Y.

Subtract P.M.   −____ = SECOND MINOR CHALLENGE

Digit (1)

Subtract digit (2)   −____

                        = MAJOR CHALLENGE

Additional challenge only if the digit found is different from those above.

P.M.

Subtract Month   −____

Reduce   = ADDITIONAL MINOR CHALLENGE

Personal Day: (P.M. + Day)   Day you are using _____ . Its digit _____ .

P.M.   ____ (Personal Month Digit)

Plus Day Digit   +____

Total   = ____ + ____ = ____ P.D. (Personal Day)

PERSONAL DAY PINNACLES

Digit of Calendar Month you are using _____ .

                                          Duration:

(1)

P.M.

Add Day   +__

Reduce   = __ + __ = __ From midnight to 6 A.M.

(2)

P.M.

Add P.D.   +__

Reduce   = __ + __ = __ From 6 A.M. to noon.

(3)

Digit (1)

Add digit (2)   +__

Reduce   = __ + __ = __ From noon to 6 P.M.

(4)

Day

Add P.D.   +__

Reduce   = __ + __ = __ From 6 P.M. to midnight.

PERSONAL DAY CHALLENGES

(subtract smaller digit from larger digit.)

P.M.

Subtract Day   −___

= 1st MINOR CHALLENGE

P.M.

Subtract P.D.   −___

= 2nd MINOR CHALLENGE

Digit (1)

Subtract digit (2)   −___

= MAJOR CHALLENGE

Additional challenge only if different from the three Personal Day Challenges above.

Day

Subtract P.D.   −___

= ADDITIONAL MINOR CHALLENGE

Personal Hours can be found in the same way. Universal Hour "1" is from midnight to 1 A.M. Universal Hours run on a 24-hour cycle so the hour from noon to 1 P.M. would be a 13 Universal Hour, etc., and the hour from 11 P.M. to midnight would be the 24th hour. To find the Personal Hour you add the Universal Hour (U.H.) to the Personal Day digit and reduce if necessary.

PERSONAL HOUR:

Select the Universal Hour you wish to use. ____A.M.____P.M. U.H. Its Digit ____.

          P.D.

      Add U.H. +___

        Total   = __ + __ = __ P.H. (Personal Hour).

PERSONAL HOUR PINNACLES
(four cycles of 15 minutes each)

(1)   Duration

         P.D.

      Add U.H. +___

      Reduce   = __ + __ = __ From hour to 15 minutes after.

(2)

         P.D.

      Add P.H. +___

      Reduce   = __ + __ = __ 15 minutes after to half past.

(3)

      Digit(1)

    Add digit (2) +___

      Reduce   = __ + __ = __ Half past till quarter to the hour.

(4)

        U.H.

      Add P.H. +___

      Reduce   = __ + __ = __ Quarter till to the hour.

PERSONAL HOUR CHALLENGES

(Use single digits only)

U.H.

Subtract P.D. −___

= FIRST MINOR CHALLENGE

P.H.

Subtract P.D. −___

= SECOND MINOR CHALLENGE

Digit (1)

Subtract digit (2) −___

= MAJOR CHALLENGE

U.H.

Subtract P.H. −___

= ADDITIONAL MINOR CHALLENGE

EXPRESSION, SOUL URGE, QUIETSELF

SU digits: __   +   __   +   __   =   __ SU

SU subtotals:

VOWELS:

FULL NAME: _____   _____   _____

NUMERIC VALUES:

EXPR subtotals;   __   __   __

EXPR digits: +   +   =   =   __ EXPR

CONSONANTS:

QS subtotals: __   __   __

QS digits: +   +   =   =   __ QS

SOUL URGE CHALLENGE _____QUIET SELF CHALLENGE _____EXPRESSION CHALLENGE.

INCLUSION FORM

Using the numeric value fo each letter in the full name, add the total in each number group as follows, placing a 0 on the line of missing numbers.

Letters having a numeric value of 1: __
Letters having a numeric value of 2: __
Letters having a numeric value of 3: __
Letters having a numeric value of 4: __
Letters having a numeric value of 5: __
Letters having a numeric value of 6: __
Letters having a numeric value of 7: __
Letters having a numeric value of 8: __
Letters having a numeric value of 9: __

Total (same as number of letters in the full name) ____

INCLUSION CHART

Place the grouping of the letters from the full name in the correct square of the Inclusion Chart below. If a number is missing, place a 0 in that square. See the proper placement on the left.

1's	2's	3's
4's	5's	6's
7's	8's	9's

RULING PASSION

From the Inclusion chart above, the square(s) having the highest total:

_____ _____ _____ _____

RULING PASSION CHALLENGES

Use the Inclusion chart again to note which number(s) are missing or have a 0. The missing number(s) denote a challenge.

____ ____ ____ ____

EXCUSION CHART

AGE	TRANSIT			LETTER VALUE			ESSENCE	P.Y.	U.Y.	YEAR
	F	M	L	F	M	L				
							=			
							=			
							=			
							=			
							=			
							=			
							=			
							=			
							=			
							=			
							=			
							=			
							=			
							=			
							=			
							=			
							=			
							=			
							=			
							=			
							=			
							=			
							=			

NOTES

NOTES

STAY IN TOUCH

On the following pages you will find some of the books now available on related subjects. Your book dealer stocks most of these and will stock new titles in the Llewellyn series as they become available. We urge your patronage.

To obtain our full catalog, to keep informed about new titles as they are released and to benefit from informative articles and helpful news, you are invited to write for our bimonthly news magazine/catalog, *Llewellyn's New Worlds of Mind and Spirit.* A sample copy is free, and it will continue coming to you at no cost as long as you are an active mail customer. Or you may subscribe for just $10.00 in the U.S.A. and Canada ($20.00 overseas, first class mail). Many bookstores also have *New Worlds* available to their customers. Ask for it.

Llewellyn's New Worlds of Mind and Spirit
P.O. Box 64383-056, St. Paul, MN 55164-0383, U.S.A.
* * *

TO ORDER BOOKS AND TAPES

If your book dealer does not have the books described, you may order them directly from the publisher by sending full price in U.S. funds, plus $3.00 for postage and handling for orders *under* $10.00; $4.00 for orders *over* $10.00. There are no postage and handling charges for orders over $50.00. Postage and handling rates are subject to change. We ship UPS whenever possible. Delivery guaranteed. Provide your street address as UPS does not deliver to P.O. Boxes. Allow 4-6 weeks for delivery. UPS to Canada requires a $50.00 minimum order. Orders outside the U.S.A. and Canada: Airmail—add retail price of book; add $5.00 for each non-book item (tapes, etc.); add $1.00 per item for surface mail.

FOR GROUP STUDY AND PURCHASE

Because there is a great deal of interest in group discussion and study of the subject matter of this book, we offer a special quantity price to group leaders or agents. Our special quantity price for a minimum order of five copies of *Numerology* is $32.85 cash-with-order. This price includes postage and handling within the United States. Minnesota residents must add 6.5% sales tax. For additional quantities, please order in multiples of five. For Canadian and foreign orders, add postage and handling charges as above. Credit card (VISA, MasterCard, American Express) orders are accepted. Charge card orders only ($15.00 minimum order) may be phoned in free within the U.S.A. or Canada by dialing 1-800-THE-MOON. For customer service, call 1-612-291-1970. Mail orders to:

LLEWELLYN PUBLICATIONS
P.O. Box 64383-056, St. Paul, MN 55164-0383, U.S.A.

INSTANT HANDWRITING ANALYSIS
A Key to Personal Success
by Ruth Gardner

For those who wish to increase self-awareness and begin to change some unfavorable aspect of their personality, graphology is a key to success. It can help open our inner selves and explore options for behavior change. With practice, one can make graphology an objective method for giving feedback to the self. And it is an unbeatable channel for monitoring your personal progress.

Author Ruth Gardner makes the process quick and easy, illustrating how letters are broken down vertically into three distinctive zones that help you explore your higher philosophies, daily activities and primal drives. She also explains how the size, slant, connecting strokes, spacing, and amounts of pressure all say something about the writer. Also included are sections on doodles and social graphology.

Instant Handwriting Analysis provides information for anyone interested in pursuing graphology as a hobby or career. It lists many resources for continuing study, including national graphology organizations and several correspondence schools.

0-87542-251-9, 159 pgs., 7 x 10, illus., softcover $12.00

PALMISTRY
The Whole View
by Judith Hipskind

Here is a unique approach to palmistry! Judy Hipskind not only explains how to analyze hands, but also explains why hand analysis works. The approach is based on a practical rationale and is easy to understand. Over 130 illustrations accompany the informal, positive view of hand analysis.

This new approach to palmistry avoids categorical predictions and presents the meaning of the palm as a synthesis of many factors: the shape, gestures, flexibility, mounts and lives of each hand—as well as a combination of the effects of both heredity and the environment. No part of the hand is treated as a separate unit; the hand reflects the entire personality. An analysis based on the method presented in this book is a rewarding experience for the client—a truly whole view!

0-87542-306-X, 248 pgs., 5-1/4 x 8, illus., softcover $8.95